The Internet

The Inter-net

How to get connected and explore the World Wide Web, exchange news and e-mail, download software, and communicate on-line.

A DK PUBLISHING BOOK

Conceived, edited, and designed by DK Direct Limited

Project Editor Brian Cooper
Art Editor Nigel Coath

Editors Anna Milner, Terry Burrows
Senior Designer Tim Mann

Text Contributors Brian Cooper, Anna Milner,
Terry Burrows, Simon Collin, Susan Schlachter, Tim Mann
Illustrators Coneyl Jay, Nigel Coath,
Steve Cummiskey, Tim Mann
Photographers Sarah Ashun, Steve Gorton
Editorial Contributor Joe Elliot
Additional Design Steve Cummiskey
Technical Consultants Chris Lewis, Thomas S. Higgins
Picture Researcher Sam Ruston
US Editor Constance M. Robinson
Production Manager Ian Paton

Publisher Jonathan Reed

First American Edition, 1996
2 4 6 8 10 9 7 5 3

*Published in the United States by
DK Publishing, Inc.
95 Madison Avenue
New York, New York 10016*

A catalog record is available from the Library of Congress

ISBN 0-7894-1288-8

Color reproduction by Triffik Technology, London
Printed and bound in Great Britain by Butler & Tanner Ltd, Frome and London

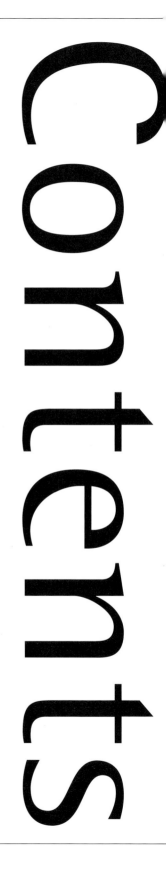

Contents

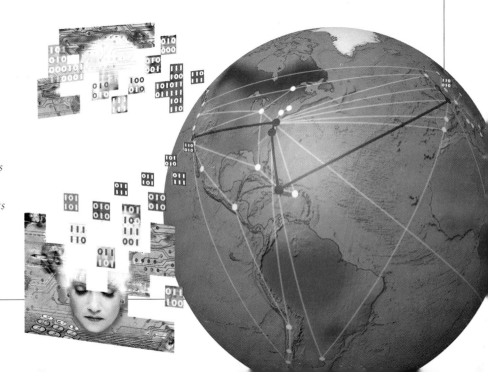

About This Book

THIS BOOK IS A BEGINNER'S GUIDE TO THE INTERNET for *Windows 95* users. It contains clear descriptions of how to connect to the Internet, how the main activities on the Internet work, and how to obtain, set up, and use all the necessary software. The book does not overload you with technical information. It tells you as much information as you need to know to make a start, and offers hands-on guidance on how to use the main areas of the Internet by means of detailed, thoroughly tested examples. It contains essential reference material, and also points you to more detailed technical information on the Internet.

Tip Boxes

Throughout this book you will find useful information in three types of tip boxes.

Question Box
Provides answers to some commonly asked questions.

Warning Box
Gives warnings about, and provides solutions for, common problems.

Supertip Box
Offers useful tips, hints, and advice.

How To Use This Book

If you don't already have an Internet connection, Chapter 1 will guide you through the most important steps on the Internet: choosing and configuring a modem, signing up with an Internet service provider, and configuring your *Windows 95* software to connect to the Internet. You should work carefully through the opening chapter before using the rest of the book.

Each subsequent chapter features a particular Internet activity, such as electronic mail or the World Wide Web. You can work through these chapters in sequence, or explore the areas you are interested in first, returning to the book later to try out another area of the Internet. Once you have tried an activity for the first time, you will quickly develop a feel for how it (and the whole of the Internet) works. Each chapter introduces an activity, explains how it works, shows examples of how to access it using a popular freeware or shareware program, and tells you where to look on the Internet for related material.

NEXT STOP, THE INTERNET

This guide will be your springboard to the Internet. Once you are connected, you will find more software and reference material than you know what to do with. On the Internet, you will be able to talk, exchange information, and even play games with other users around the world. This book shows you where to go, how to get there, how the procedures work, and how to operate the most essential tools. It doesn't take long to master the basics: the rest is up to you. There is a vast electronic world waiting for you. Use this book and you will soon be able to access this world from your desktop.

Using the Reference Section

❑ **Appendix 1 – The On-Line Services**
Since many on-line services offer customer-only content as well as Internet access, we give a brief description of three leading on-line service providers.

❑ **Appendix 2 – Common File Types**
If you have problems dealing with compressed or encoded files from the Internet, refer to this section.

❑ **Appendix 3 – Troubleshooting**
Refer to the troubleshooting advice given here if you have difficulty connecting to an Internet site.

❑ **Appendix 4 – Useful Web Sites**
Refer to this Appendix for a list of sites that provide the latest Internet news as well as hundreds of useful links to beginner's guides and software sites.

❑ **Glossary**
Look up definitions of the most common Internet terms here.

How This Book Shows Internet Addresses

All the software featured in this book can be downloaded from the Internet. Throughout the book, you will see addresses of Internet sites from which you can download these and other popular Internet programs. In the software section of Appendix 4, you will find a list of software sites that contain thousands of free and try-before-you-buy Internet programs.

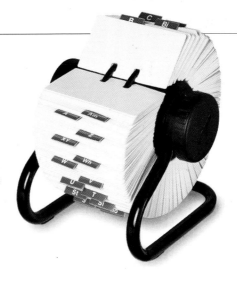

E-MAIL ADDRESSES
For example, **dave@provider.com**
All e mail addresses in this book are clearly recognizable because they contain the @ symbol.

WEB ADDRESSES
For example, **http//:www.dk.com**
All Web addresses in this book are preceded by **http://**

OTHER ADDRESSES
For example, **ftp.microsoft.com** (FTP site) and **cwis.usc.edu** (Gopher site)

There is one very important thing to note about these addresses. Internet addresses rarely end in a period. Where you see an Internet address followed by a period in this book, it is purely because of sentence punctuation. Therefore, you should ALWAYS omit the final period when typing any of the Internet addresses shown in this book.

A Final Recommendation

Using the Internet can soon become as natural as looking up information in a book, making a phone call, or visiting a store, and often it's faster and more convenient. Nevertheless, the Internet is still in its youth, and as computer networking environments evolve, unforeseen problems may arise. For this reason we recommend that you:

❏ Always use a virus checker
after downloading new applications

❏ Do not disable security features in
your Web browser (see page 75)

❏ Read all messages on Internet sites
before proceeding with any activity

These precautions are easy to overlook,
but we recommend that you don't!

What You Need To Use This Book

AN IBM-COMPATIBLE PC
with at least a 486 processor and 8 MB RAM (16 MB recommended)

Many people access the Internet with slower PCs, but you will not be able to access effectively many of the features described in this book on slower PCs.

WINDOWS 95
Windows 95 *contains all the software you need to connect to the Internet via a service provider. Once you have connected, you can download other software, such as a Web browser, for specific Internet activities.*

A MODEM
14.4K minimum,
28.8K recommended.

Chapter 1 advises you on how to choose and install a modem, and how to choose and sign up with an Internet service provider.

A TELEPHONE LINE
You need a telephone line to dial in to a service provider via a modem.

A VIRUS CHECKER
If you don't already have one, you can download a shareware version from the Internet when you are connected (see the software section of Appendix 4).

Introduction

What Is the Internet?

The Internet is the biggest computer system in the world. It is an enormous network of networks that spans the globe, continuously evolving and redefining itself. This chapter gives a brief introduction to the Internet: its history, its global nature, and the main activities that are available to anyone with a modem, a telephone line, and a suitable Internet connection.

It also gives a broad overview of the physical nature of the Internet, describing how data travels from your modem via high-speed networks to computers anywhere in the world, and the different types of software you need to join in this worldwide phenomenon.

What Is the Internet?

THE INTERNET IS A GLOBAL NETWORK OF COMPUTERS that allows many millions of computer users to share and exchange information. Hundreds of thousands of computers linked to the Internet hold vast quantities of data that you can access from your PC whenever you want to, wherever you are. Whether at home, at work, or while traveling, you have global access. If you are connecting to the Internet in the US, for example, it's just as easy to view information stored on another computer in the UK or Italy as it is to view what's stored on a computer in your home town.

What Do I Need to Know?

You don't have to be a computer expert to use the Internet. You probably use your telephone or television most days with little thought of the communication networks that send and transmit the words or images to and from your home. Within a short while, your main concern will be deciding what you want to do on the Internet rather than how to do it. The world is yours to visit – you just tell your software what to do and where to go. Most new users spend a lot of time exploring at first, just following their mood. As they become more experienced, they find themselves regularly visiting the same areas of the Net – maybe to communicate with people who share their interests, to access up-to-date information on their chosen subject, or perhaps to download some new software from a favorite site.

MAKING A START
You don't need to understand exactly how the Internet works to use it, but a little background knowledge can be helpful. This chapter looks briefly at the physical structure of the Internet and describes the basic processes. With this book, a PC running *Windows 95*, and a telephone line, you are already halfway to becoming an Internet user. You need to do just three things: install a modem, acquire some Internet software, and open an account with a local Internet service provider. It is even possible to do all this in one step. Chapter One will help you through this procedure.

FIRST STEPS ON THE NET
Many new users take a little time to feel comfortable with the enormous scale of the Internet and are often afraid of doing something that will declare "I am a newbie" to the Internet community. This fear is usually groundless. Most experienced Internet users can remember their first steps into the unknown and are generally willing to help. Although there are certain codes of behavior to bear in mind, this book will make you aware of them as you go along.

Internet Provider
An Internet service provider supplies your gateway to the Internet. The provider gives you access to the Internet, an e-mail address, a local telephone access number, and technical support.

Your PC and Modem
You access the Internet from your PC, connected by a modem to a service provider.

In the Driver's Seat
The beauty of the Internet is that it can be very simple to use. Once you have set up your Internet connection, all you need to consider is how best to use the Internet software on your PC and how to organize your visits to the Net.

What Can I Do on the Internet?

Once you are connected to the Internet, you become part of a worldwide electronic community of over 50 million users that you can communicate with in a number of ways. The Internet also comprises millions of computers holding publicly accessible software and documents. Here are five of the main Internet activities to try:

☐ Electronic Mail

You can send messages to anyone who has an Internet account. The messages can simply be text, or they may contain pictures or even spreadsheet files, and they will be stored until the recipient next logs in. E-mail is a fast and economical way to communicate globally (see pages 44-53).

☐ Transfer Files or FTP

The Internet contains gigabytes of software and millions of files that you can access easily using a process called FTP (file transfer protocol). This allows you to log on to a publicly accessible computer and download files from it onto your hard disk (see pages 42-7).

☐ Join Discussion Groups

Use the Internet to discuss your favorite subjects. You can participate in over 15,000 special discussion groups (see pages 86-93). You can also join a mailing list on a particular subject and have any new information sent to you automatically (see page 54).

☐ World Wide Web

The pages of the World Wide Web (WWW) show the colorful and innovative face of the Internet. By clicking on words, pictures, and icons, you can navigate from one site to the next quickly and simply. Hundreds of new and exciting areas appear each week on every subject that you can imagine. Many pages have multimedia features, such as video and sound. To access the Web you need to use Web browser software, with a modem, which enables you to carry out nearly every Internet activity from within one program (see pages 56-79).

☐ Communicate Live

If you feel like having a conversation or playing a game over the Internet with another Net user, there are many ways of doing so. Chatting (conversing via your keyboard in real time) is very popular. Head-to-head games have always been popular – on the Internet there are many areas devoted to multiplayer games (see pages 94-107).

Other Users

Other Internet users may be connected to the same provider as you, or to one of the thousands of similar Internet providers worldwide. These users can connect using almost any type of computer.

The Network of Networks

At its simplest, a network is a pair of computers linked together by cable so that they can share information, hardware (such as printers), and programs. The Internet is the biggest network of all – millions of computers linked together by standard telephone lines, fiberoptic cables, and satellite and microwave links. At the core of the Internet is a network of powerful mainframe computers – known as supercomputers – located at sites all over the world. These machines are connected by high-speed links, which are known as "backbones."

For the majority of ordinary users, access to the Internet comes in the form of commercial service providers who run powerful computer systems connected to the supercomputer backbone. With a personal computer, a modem, and an account with one of the service providers, subscribers simply dial in and connect their computers using a standard telephone line.

Evolution of the Internet

The Internet began in 1969 when the US Department of Defense commissioned the Advanced Research Project Agency to create ARPANET – a huge military computer network. They came up with a system which sent information broken down into "packets" of data. This system (Transmission Control Protocol/Internet Protocol, or TCP/IP) allowed data to move freely around the military network. This meant that if one of its computers became damaged, the data would be able to arrive safely by finding alternative routes. In the early 1980s the American military split away from ARPANET, leaving what became known as the Internet. Academic institutions and other government agencies, such as NSFNet (National Science Foundation Network), soon joined the Internet, connecting their own computer networks to the system.

The Giant Network

The main network in the US is the NSFNet, which was originally created by the National Science Foundation in New York. This is shown as white lines on the illustration below. Each of the main dots is a supercomputer which routes information between itself and the other supercomputers along the high-speed backbones. Each node is linked to a number of smaller regional networks, which are in turn linked to yet smaller networks, and eventually to your PC.

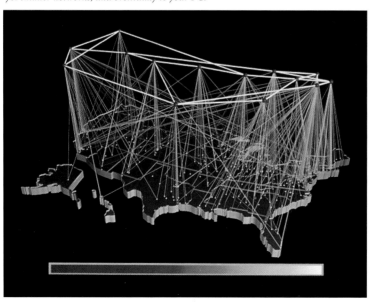

Is the Net Worldwide?
Technically, yes. Anyone with a PC and modem can telephone an Internet provider and access the Net. Some countries (certain African countries, for example) currently have few Internet service providers and local coverage can be limited. This can entail expensive long-distance calls before users can connect to the Internet. Another important consideration is the level of sophistication of a country's telephone system.

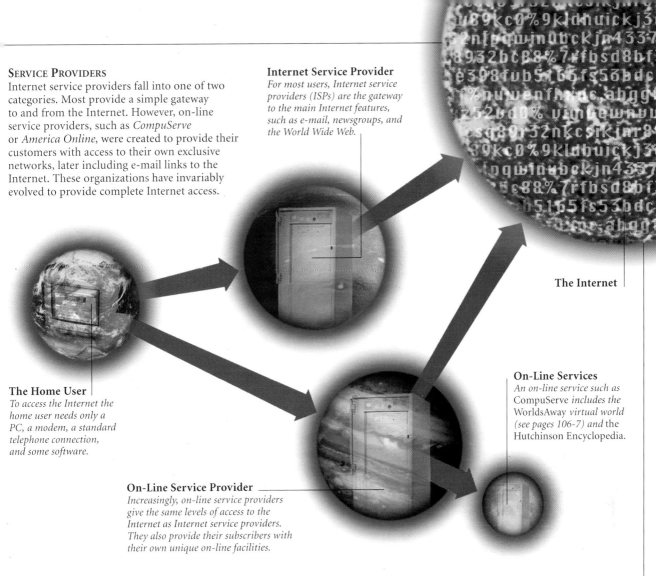

SERVICE PROVIDERS

Internet service providers fall into one of two categories. Most provide a simple gateway to and from the Internet. However, on-line service providers, such as *CompuServe* or *America Online*, were created to provide their customers with access to their own exclusive networks, later including e-mail links to the Internet. These organizations have invariably evolved to provide complete Internet access.

Internet Service Provider
For most users, Internet service providers (ISPs) are the gateway to the main Internet features, such as e-mail, newsgroups, and the World Wide Web.

The Internet

On-Line Services
An on-line service such as CompuServe *includes the* WorldsAway *virtual world (see pages 106-7) and the* Hutchinson Encyclopedia.

The Home User
To access the Internet the home user needs only a PC, a modem, a standard telephone connection, and some software.

On-Line Service Provider
Increasingly, on-line service providers give the same levels of access to the Internet as Internet service providers. They also provide their subscribers with their own unique on-line facilities.

How Data Moves Around

From your personal computer, information is sent down the telephone line via a modem. This is a separate piece of hardware that converts digital information into an analog audio signal – the kind used for telephone traffic. The signal is received by the service provider and routed through to the Internet backbone. Each message transmitted from your computer is converted into TCP/IP packets, each one of which reaches its destination via a series of network interconnections. Each time a packet passes through a "router" or "bridge" connecting two networks, the router checks that the information in the packet is intact. If it isn't, the router asks for the packet to be sent again. This transfer process is known as "packet switching."

Packet Switching
Information passing across the Internet between any two PCs is broken down into "packets" of data. Each individual packet may travel along very different routes before being joined together at the final destination.

First Steps on the Internet

MANY BEGINNERS FIND THEIR FIRST EXPERIENCE OF THE INTERNET overwhelming. Faced with the wide range of activities available and the scope and magnitude of the information resources, new users spend a lot of time simply finding their bearings. However, it soon becomes clear that the Internet is similar to any other medium of information or communication. Once you know the information you want to find, how to find it, and how to access it, the Internet becomes an extremely powerful resource – whether you use it for work, education, entertainment, communication, or just for the fun of exploring.

Visiting Internet Sites
If you know the address of a specific site you want to visit (such as DK's site at **www.dk.com**), *you simply type it here and press the Return key. You might need to type the full address, by including* **http://** *at the beginning.*

How Do I Get There?

Before you can decide how you want to use the Internet, you need to have a good idea of what is "out there." For beginners, the best starting point is to use one of the powerful Web browsers currently available, such as *Netscape Navigator* from Netscape Communications Corporation or Microsoft's *Internet Explorer.* Many service providers supply you with a Web browser when you register an account (and sometimes when you take out a trial account).

Since the early days, Web browsers have been used mainly to access the pages of the World Wide Web. By clicking on a "hypertext" link on the page (usually some highlighted text, an image, or a button) it is possible to jump from one Internet site to another, regardless of its location – an activity often referred to as "surfing the Internet."

But today's powerful browsers are much more versatile and allow you to try nearly all the activities that are possible on the Internet.

EXPLORING THE INTERNET WITH A WEB BROWSER
Throughout this book you will see detailed descriptions of each of the Net's main features and many examples of Internet software. The examples on the right show how you can use a Web browser - in this case, *Netscape Navigator* - to perform many of these Internet activities. With this program you can:

- ❏ Visit Web sites
- ❏ Send and receive electronic mail
- ❏ Read and post articles in newsgroups
- ❏ Transfer files and programs from publicly accessible sites to your PC
- ❏ Chat with other users on-line
- ❏ Play games with other on-line gamers
- ❏ Access on-line multimedia (including live radio and video broadcasts)
- ❏ Use powerful on-line tools for searching the Internet
- ❏ Go shopping on-line

WEB BROWSER
Because Web pages are produced using hypertext, you can quickly move from one place to another within a document, or from that page to any other linked document regardless of where it is on the Internet. With *Netscape Navigator* you can access millions of pages simply by clicking on "hot" text and images.

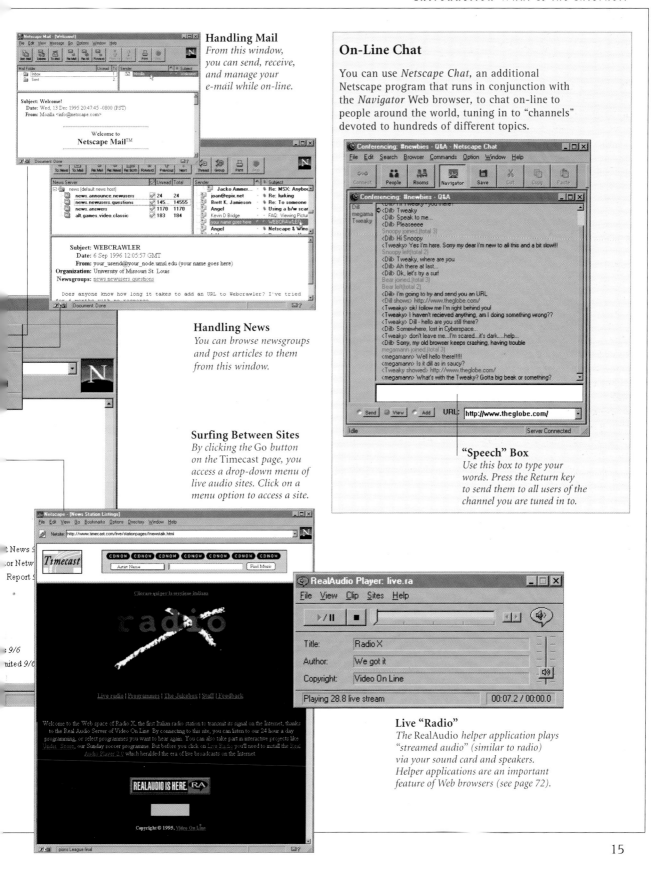

Handling Mail
*From this window,
you can send, receive,
and manage your
e-mail while on-line.*

Handling News
*You can browse newsgroups
and post articles to them
from this window.*

Surfing Between Sites
*By clicking the Go button
on the Timecast page, you
access a drop-down menu of
live audio sites. Click on a
menu option to access a site.*

On-Line Chat

You can use *Netscape Chat*, an additional
Netscape program that runs in conjunction with
the *Navigator* Web browser, to chat on-line to
people around the world, tuning in to "channels"
devoted to hundreds of different topics.

"Speech" Box
*Use this box to type your
words. Press the Return key
to send them to all users of the
channel you are tuned in to.*

Live "Radio"
*The RealAudio helper application plays
"streamed audio" (similar to radio)
via your sound card and speakers.
Helper applications are an important
feature of Web browsers (see page 72).*

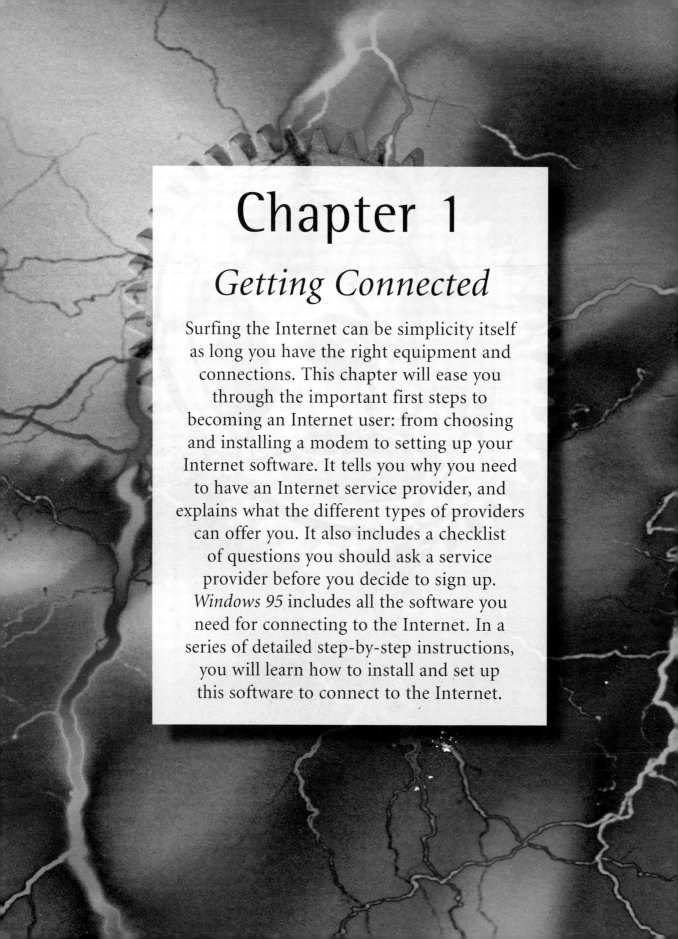

Chapter 1

Getting Connected

Surfing the Internet can be simplicity itself
as long you have the right equipment and
connections. This chapter will ease you
through the important first steps to
becoming an Internet user: from choosing
and installing a modem to setting up your
Internet software. It tells you why you need
to have an Internet service provider, and
explains what the different types of providers
can offer you. It also includes a checklist
of questions you should ask a service
provider before you decide to sign up.
Windows 95 includes all the software you
need for connecting to the Internet. In a
series of detailed step-by-step instructions,
you will learn how to install and set up
this software to connect to the Internet.

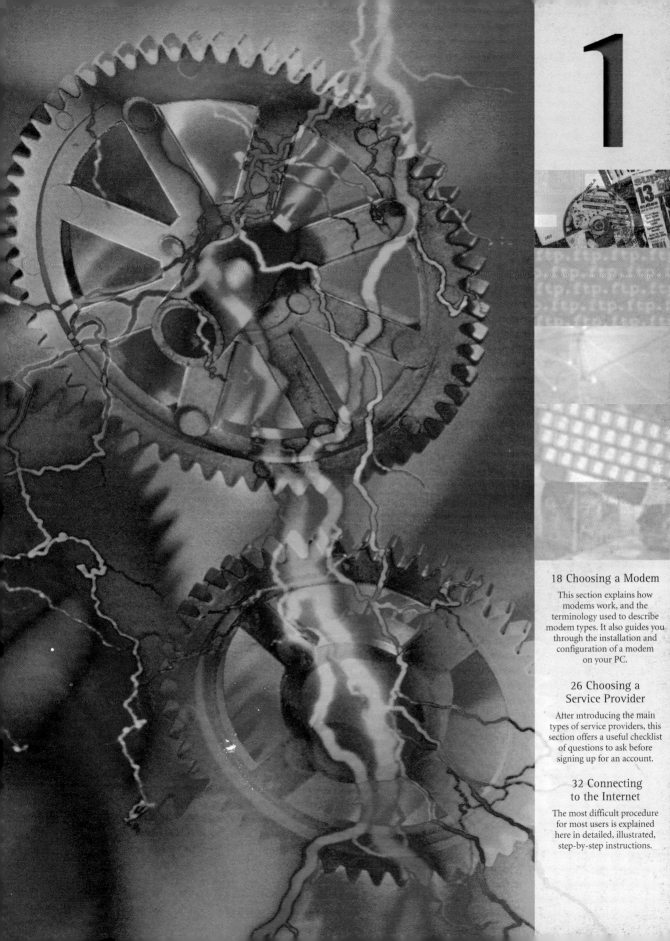

1

Choosing a Modem

To CONNECT TO THE INTERNET OR COMMUNICATE with other computers or on-line services, you need a modem. Modems are devices for translating data from binary code (the string of zeros and ones that your computer reads and interprets) to analog data that can be transmitted over the telephone network. When telephone lines eventually all become digital, the modem will become unnecessary, although you will still need an ISDN adapter (see tip box). Until then, you need a modem to use the Internet, to dial in to bulletin board and commercial on-line services, and to send and receive e-mail and fax messages.

Transfer Speeds
The speed at which a modem is capable of transferring data is measured in bits per second (bps). The most suitable modems for regular Internet use are capable of 14,400 bps or 28,800 bps. These modems can also be described as 14.4K and 28.8K respectively.

What Is a Modem?

Modems come in many shapes and sizes but they all perform the same basic function. The word "modem" is a contraction of MOdulator–DEModulator. Modulation describes the conversion of data from binary to analog; demodulation describes the process in reverse. In other words, when you send a document from your PC to a friend's, it is converted to an analog signal by your modem and converted back to binary when it arrives at your friend's modem. A similar procedure occurs if you choose to send a fax from your PC to a fax machine.

External Modem
One of the advantages of an external modem is that you can quickly check the status of your modem by looking at the display lights on the case (see pages 22-3).

FAX-MODEMS
Most modems today are capable of sending and receiving faxes. Such modems are usually (but not always) called fax-modems. While the manufacturer will usually supply some software, *Windows 95* already contains several modem utilities, including a fax program (called *Microsoft Fax*), that you can use to send and receive faxes.

Connecting Cable

Modem Software

Modem Manual

Fax-Modem

ALL-IN-ONE INTERNET KITS
Boxed "starter" packs are becoming increasingly popular for beginners. Many contain a modem, cable and adapter, software, and a manual. Some also offer a free trial account with a reputable service provider.

How Modems Work

This illustration shows how a modem transforms binary data sent from your computer. It shows data (an e-mail message, for example) en route to your service provider, but the same principle applies to data sent to any modem or fax device.

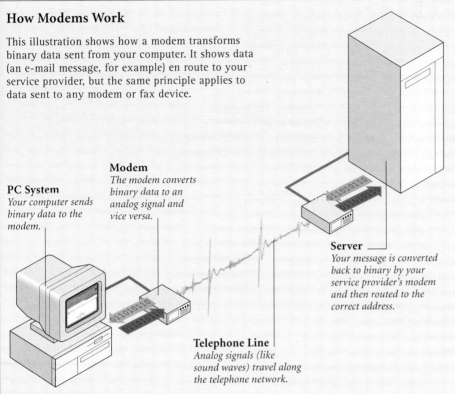

PC System
Your computer sends binary data to the modem.

Modem
The modem converts binary data to an analog signal and vice versa.

Server
Your message is converted back to binary by your service provider's modem and then routed to the correct address.

Telephone Line
Analog signals (like sound waves) travel along the telephone network.

Choosing a Modem

Once you've decided which sort of modem you need in terms of speed, price, and compatibility, read some reviews in a current Internet or PC magazine before buying. If you are very short of desk space, you will probably look for a slimline external modem, or perhaps choose an internal modem.

External Modem
The size and design of external modems can vary considerably.

Card Modem
This credit-card-sized modem is ideal for notebook PCs.

Internal Modem
An internal modem occupies an expansion slot inside your PC (see box on page 21).

What Is ISDN?

ISDN (Integrated Services Digital Network) provides the fastest link to the Internet at a price aimed at home users. ISDN transmits digital information down existing phone lines, achieving rates of between 64,000 bps and 300,000 bps. It is virtually error-free and can also be used to transmit voice. You need a special telephone connection to use ISDN, and you can only use it for accessing the Internet if your service provider also has an ISDN link. Some service providers charge higher rates for ISDN connections, but many do not.

Do I Need the Fastest Modem?

If you intend to use a modem to explore the World Wide Web and download a lot of files you should buy the fastest model you can afford. Currently your best bet is a 28.8K modem. Otherwise, a 14.4K modem is acceptable, although it will seem frustratingly slow when accessing the many multimedia and virtual reality sites on the Web. A number of other factors can affect the speed at which your modem transfers data (see pages 21-2). Faster data transfer speeds are also important for Internet users who pay telephone bills. Some communications providers allow free local calls to the Internet, but many do not.

SPEED ISN'T EVERYTHING

Some people are perfectly happy to use a slower modem, such as a 9,600 bps model, because they use it mainly for sending and receiving e-mail or accessing newsgroups — essentially text-based activities. Browsing the Web is possible with a slow modem but requires a lot of patience. It can take an extremely long time for the more graphics-intensive Web pages to appear on your monitor if you are using a slower modem. For those who need to consider the cost of telephone calls and communications surcharges, faster modems can save both time and money.

External vs. Internal Modems

Whether you choose an external or an internal modem depends on a number of factors. If you are unlikely to use your modem on another PC, or if you are short of desk space or electrical sockets, an internal modem may be your answer. Less experienced PC users may find the process of setting up an internal modem rather complicated, however. Some of the main pros and cons of choosing each type of modem are listed on the right.

An Internal Modem:

■ Takes up no additional space on the desktop

■ Does not need a serial cable or additional electrical socket

■ Has its own built-in serial port and is therefore unaffected by the UART chip problem described opposite

■ *Is more difficult to install than an external modem*

■ *May require changes to hardware settings*

An External Modem:

■ Is easy to install

■ Can be moved easily and set up on another PC

■ Uses helpful indicator lights on its case so that you can monitor the status of your Internet session

■ *May require a new serial port if using a 28.8K model on an older PC*

■ *Requires an additional electrical socket and cable*

EXTERNAL INDICATORS

Some people prefer to see the display lights on the modem case because they give a useful indication of the modem's status. A glance at the indicator lights on the case will tell you quickly whether your modem is idle, for example, or whether it is sending or receiving data. The number and nature of the display lights vary considerably, according to the modem's make and model.

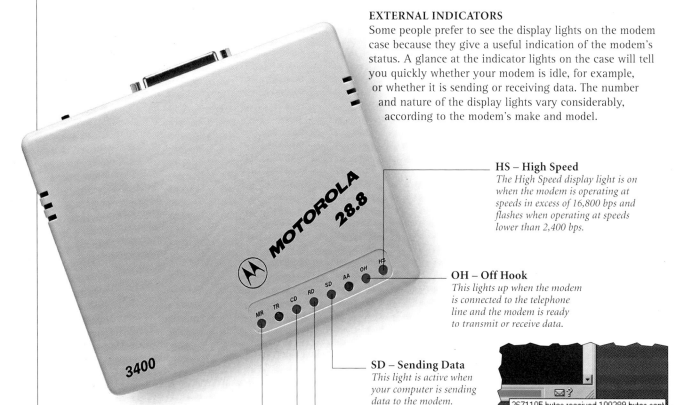

HS – High Speed
The High Speed display light is on when the modem is operating at speeds in excess of 16,800 bps and flashes when operating at speeds lower than 2,400 bps.

OH – Off Hook
This lights up when the modem is connected to the telephone line and the modem is ready to transmit or receive data.

SD – Sending Data
This light is active when your computer is sending data to the modem.

RD – Receiving Data
This lights up when your computer is receiving data from the modem.

MR – Modem Ready
This light shows that the modem is switched on and ready for use.

CD – Carrier Detect
This light is active when the modem has detected a signal from a remote modem.

DESKTOP MODEM ICON
Windows 95 displays a modem icon on the taskbar when the modem is active. During data transfer, the lights alternate between red and green. Hold the mouse pointer over this icon to see more information.

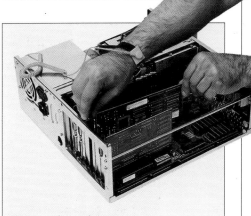

Is My Serial Port Fast Enough?

On some older PCs you may not get the most from a 28.8K modem because your serial port is too slow. The steps below show how you can check the speed of your serial port. If your serial port uses a chip called an 8250 UART (Universal Asynchronous Receiver/Transmitter), your modem will only perform as well as a 14.4K modem. To use an external 28.8K modem effectively, you need a 16550 UART chip (see tip box on this page). If your PC uses the slower type of chip, and you want to use a 28.8K modem, you can overcome the problem by installing a fast serial card in one of the expansion slots inside your computer.

Fast UART Chip
An add-on serial card with a built-in 16550 UART chip.

Internal Modems

Installing an internal modem is not recommended for beginners. An internal modem is a card that needs to be fitted into a vacant expansion slot on the PC's motherboard, carefully following the manufacturer's instructions. The process is similar to installing a sound card, for instance. Once installation is complete, the *Windows 95* set-up procedure is similar to that described on pages 23-4, but it may be necessary to make further adjustments to *Windows 95* settings.

How to Check the Speed of Your Serial Port

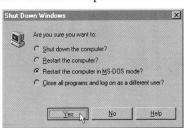

1 You first need to restart your PC in MS-DOS mode. To do this, click *Shut Down* in the *Start* menu. In the *Shut Down Windows* dialog box, check the box next to *Restart the computer in MS-DOS mode?* and click *Yes*.

2 After your PC has restarted you will see the DOS prompt (C:>). Type **msd** and press Return. This will run Microsoft's diagnostics utility. Now click the *COM Ports* button. (If your mouse is temporarily disabled, simply press the C key instead.)

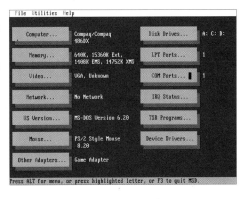

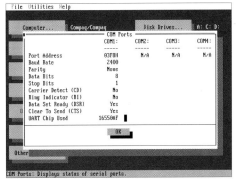

3 Read the information on the *UART Chip Used* line. If you can see the number 16550, you have a fast enough serial port to run a 28.8K modem effectively. If you see only 8250, you will need to consider an upgrade. Consult your PC supplier for further information.

What Is a Fast UART Chip?
The 16550 UART chip is known as a "buffered" chip. In other words, it uses a buffer (a small memory block for temporarily storing data) to store information that arrives before your computer can process it. An 8250 UART chip is not buffered and its performance is likely to suffer at higher speeds – usually resulting in unreliable or slow data transfer.

21

Speed, Error Correction, and Data Compression Standards

It is important to make sure that your modem can send data accurately, without errors, as well as rapidly. When you speak on the phone you may sometimes hear hisses and crackles; these can corrupt data transmission and cause problems. To get over this "electrical noise" on the telephone line, modems should include error correction features. There are two popular systems: MNP (Microcom Networking Protocol) and V.42.

Data Compression

Data compression is also an important consideration when buying a modem. This does exactly what it says: it compresses data as it is being transmitted. The most common form of data compression is V.42bis. This can quadruple the effective rate at which data is sent by the modem. The faster you send data, the more the modem is prone to noise, so error correction is vital for high-speed modems, but less important for low-speed modems.

Some Important Modem Standards

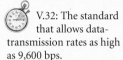 V.32: The standard that allows data-transmission rates as high as 9,600 bps.

 V.34: A standard that supports transmission at 28,800 bps.

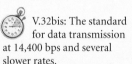 V.32bis: The standard for data transmission at 14,400 bps and several slower rates.

V.42: A standard for error correction based on the LAPM standard, which also can use MNP Classes 2-4.

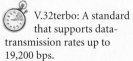 V.32terbo: A standard that supports data-transmission rates up to 19,200 bps.

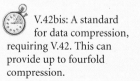 V.42bis: A standard for data compression, requiring V.42. This can provide up to fourfold compression.

How to Connect and Install an External Modem

Connecting a modem to your PC is usually a quick and easy task. First connect your modem's power supply unit to the mains. Then connect your modem to the PC using one of the vacant serial ports. Attach one end of the serial cable to your modem, then the other end to a vacant serial port on your PC. This will usually be the COM 1 port although, if a mouse is already connected here, you can use COM 2. Finally, plug the telephone cable into a telephone socket and switch on your modem. Some of the lights on the case should light up.

DON'T FORGET THE CABLE
When buying a modem, ask whether a serial cable is supplied. It is helpful to note the size of the serial port you intend using (you refer to them in terms of pins; e.g. 25-pin or 9-pin). When you buy your modem, get the supplier to confirm that the cable you buy will fit your PC, or ask for a suitable adapter plug.

Serial Cable Adapter
Adapter cables or plugs are available for converting a 25-pin plug to fit a 9-pin socket. These adapters are available for mouse or modem. Make sure you use a modem adapter.

AC Power Adapter
Some modems have an adapter cable attached to the case. Others have a jack that you plug in to the modem's case.

Connecting an External Modem

First connect the serial cable between the socket on your modem and a serial port on the back of your PC. Usually there is only one suitable serial port available – your mouse is usually plugged into the other. Then connect the telephone cable to a telephone socket. Finally, connect the power supply cable between your modem and the main power supply using the power adapter, if one is supplied with your modem.

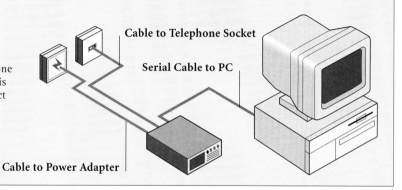

Cable to Telephone Socket

Serial Cable to PC

Cable to Power Adapter

Using Windows 95 to Configure an External Modem

Once you have have correctly connected an external modem to your PC (see opposite), you are ready to configure it in *Windows 95*. Before you begin, make sure that the modem is connected to the power supply and switched on. At least one of the display lights on the modem case should be on. Although it is possible to let *Windows 95* detect the make and model of your modem automatically, the process is quicker if you select these details manually when following the steps below. If you encounter any difficulties, see "Modem Troubleshooting" on page 24.

1 From the *Start* button, go to *Settings* and then *Control Panel.*

Noisy Modem Problems?
If the screechy sound that a modem makes when it establishes a connection sets your teeth on edge, you might consider buying an internal modem, or an external modem that has a volume control built-in to the case. Although there are several ways of disabling this sound on external modems – by changing software or hardware settings – it's simpler to use a modem with automatic volume control.

2 Double-click the *Modems* icon. The *Install New Modem* box will appear.

3 Follow the instructions in the box, and then check the box next to *Don't detect my modem; I will select it from a list.* Then click *Next.*

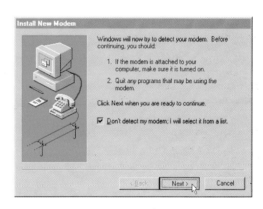

4 Using the vertical scroll bars, select the appropriate make and model of your modem in the *Manufacturers* box and then the *Models* box. Then click *Next.*

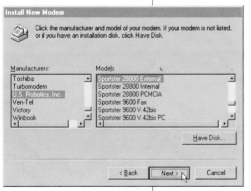

5 Choose the appropriate port in the *Select the port to use with this modem* panel, then click *Next.* Click *Finish* when the message box appears.

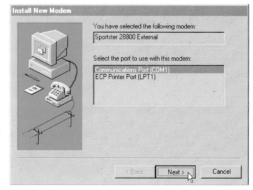

6 In the *Modems Properties* box that appears, on the *General* page, click the *Dialing Properties* button.

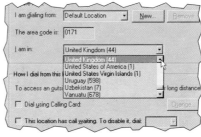

7 Type the appropriate information in the box next to *The area code is*. Then click the arrow on the right of the box next to *I am in*, and choose your country from the drop-down list. Click *OK* and, finally, click *OK* in the *Modems Properties* dialog box. Your modem is now ready to use.

Modem Troubleshooting

Windows 95 supports hundreds of different modems, but not all. If your modem does not appear in the list at Step 4, you have several options. You could repeat the steps above and let *Windows 95* try to autodetect your modem. It will probably choose *Standard Modem Types* and the appropriate speed. This will usually get you up and running, but you should ask your supplier whether *Windows 95*-compatible modem drivers are available for the model you have bought. Alternatively, if you have a disk containing a *Windows 95* driver supplied with your modem, follow the steps above, but click the *Have disk* button at Step 4, navigate to the floppy disk drive, and click on the appropriate file. Then follow Steps 5-7 above.

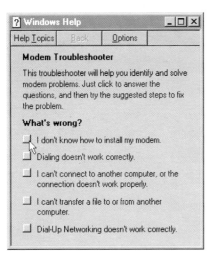

STILL HAVING PROBLEMS?
Windows 95 offers on-line help on how to install your modem. Access *Windows Help* (see "Additional Solutions" on the right) and click on *I don't know how to install my modem*. This will take you directly through the procedure described in the steps above.

Disable Call Waiting!
If you use "call waiting" with your telephone, you should disable it during modem sessions. The beep that announces an incoming call could disrupt data transfer. To do this, check the box next to *This location has call waiting* in the *Dialing Properties* dialog box (see Step 7 on the left). You will also need to contact your phone company to find out what to put in the box next to *To disable it, dial*.

Additional Solutions

The *Windows 95* help system contains useful advice on modem problems. To access this, choose *Help* from the *Start* menu, double-click *Troubleshooting* in the *Contents* page, then double-click on *If you have trouble using your modem*.

How to Find Modem Drivers

Look on the Manufacturer's Disks
Windows 95-compatible drivers may be available on the disks supplied with your modem.

Look on the Windows CD
Some additional modem drivers are supplied with the Windows 95 upgrade CD-ROM.

Call the Supplier
When in doubt, call your modem supplier. The supplier should be able to advise you on any problems regarding Windows 95-compatible modem drivers.

Dialing Out with Your Modem

Now your modem is configured, you may want to test it immediately by dialing in to a local Bulletin Board Service (BBS). You do not need an Internet connection to use a BBS; all you need is a telephone number for the BBS and the *Windows 95* accessory called *HyperTerminal*.

Developed for Microsoft by Hilgraeve Inc.   Copyright © 1995 Hilgraeve Inc.

INSTALLING HYPERTERMINAL
If you can't find *HyperTerminal* on your PC, you can install it from your *Windows 95* installation CD or disks, using the *Add/Remove Programs* Control Panel utility.

USING HYPERTERMINAL
When you make a connection to a remote computer or bulletin board for the first time, *HyperTerminal* prompts you for information about dialing properties and modem settings, enabling you to assign an icon and a name to each connection. The next time you need to make a particular connection, all you have to do is double-click the relevant icon in the *HyperTerminal* window.

You will find a number of BBSs advertised in computer magazines. Most services are text-based and can be accessed via your *HyperTerminal* window. Once you have connected to a BBS, you need to follow carefully any instructions on your screen. You may also need to register some personal details. If you decide you don't want to proceed at any point, it is easy to disconnect from a BBS: you simply cancel the session by clicking the *Disconnect* icon on the *HyperTerminal* window toolbar.

What Is a BBS?

A Bulletin Board Service is essentially a computer, with a modem attached, that allows other PC users to access information on it. Many BBSs are commercial concerns; many others are free services run by specialists, enthusiasts, or games-players. Depending on the type of BBS, users can read and post messages to discussion groups, download software from the BBS to their PCs, play on-line games, and "talk" with other users via the keyboard.

Beware of the Bill!
You will normally pay connection charges (usually a by-the-minute rate) when accessing commercial BBSs.

How to Connect with HyperTerminal

1 From the *Start* menu, choose *Programs*, and then *HyperTerminal* from the *Accessories* submenu. In the *HyperTerminal* window, double-click the icon labeled *Hypertrm*.

2 In the *Connection Description* dialog box, type a name in the *Name* box for the BBS you are going to call, and then click an icon in the *Icon* box. Click *OK*. The icon and name will now appear in the *HyperTerminal* window.

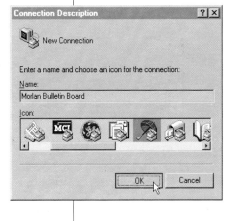

3 In the *Phone Number* dialog box, choose the relevant country code, and then type the area code and phone number for the BBS you are going to call. Click *OK*. A *Connect* box now appears. Click *Dial* to connect to the BBS.

Choosing a Service Provider

O NCE YOU HAVE BOUGHT AND INSTALLED YOUR MODEM and Internet software, your next step is to set up an account with a company that can provide you with Internet access: a service provider. Making the choice to go with a particular service provider is not easy. There are several types of service providers that will offer you different services and benefits, at different costs. Service providers usually fall into two main categories: Internet service providers (ISPs) and on-line service providers (OSPs). The main difference between an ISP and an OSP involves content and cost. All ISPs, and most OSPs, give you a connection to the Internet, but on-line service providers also provide "content" (information and services that are exclusive to that OSP). On these pages, you will see a comparison of the main features of the two types of service providers.

What Is a POP?
POPs (points of presence) are the local telephone access numbers offered by service providers. If you can dial any of these POPs at local call rates (just check the area code as you would for any telephone number), you will be able to use the Internet at that rate. The number of POPs offered by service providers varies considerably.

Internet Service Providers

Some Internet service providers simply give you a connection to the Internet and software to dial the nearest POP (see tip box) to make the Internet connection. You are then expected to download the software you need from a suitable FTP site (sometimes maintained by the service provider). Other Internet service providers include a suite of Internet programs as part of the service. This usually includes a Web browser, an e-mail program, and an FTP program.

   As far as cost is concerned, Internet service providers usually charge a sign-up fee and then a fixed monthly or annual fee for unlimited access to the Internet. Internet service providers usually do not provide additional content.

Internet Service Providers

Internet Access
If an ISP provides a direct Internet connection, you can run any Internet software, including the latest Web browsers.

On-Line Charges
Internet service providers normally charge a flat monthly or annual fee that allows you to connect to and use the Internet for as long as you like without incurring any extra charges.

No Extra Content
ISPs give you no extra content – you simply have access to the Internet as a whole. It is then up to you how you use it.

POP Coverage
The main Internet service providers normally have excellent POP coverage in their country, although it may be difficult to access your account when traveling abroad.

Look for Support!
One big selling point for any service provider is the ability to offer support to newcomers. Unfortunately, many ISPs have not been very good at providing support over the telephone, but this is improving. OSPs such as *CompuServe* and *AOL* provide telephone support free of charge. This can be invaluable for a newcomer.

Connecting with Microsoft

Microsoft offers you one of the easiest ways to connect to the Internet, mainly because the software for *The Microsoft Network* is included with *Windows 95*. Until 1996, *The Microsoft Network* operated exclusively as an on-line service. It now occupies a position somewhere between an ISP and an OSP, offering similar monthly billing to an ISP for Internet access, in some countries, but also retaining its OSP content.

Click and Register
Double-clicking this Windows 95 desktop icon takes you straight into the registration screens for MSN.

On-Line Service Providers

CompuServe and *America Online (AOL)* are two of the main on-line service providers. Both have vast databases of information covering, for example, business, weather, news, software support, and travel. They also give you Internet access via a number of easy-to-follow screens. You access FTP sites or the Web simply by clicking a button.

On-line service providers usually do not charge a sign-up fee, but your monthly charge only allows a fixed number of hours on-line (between 5 and 10). Additional time costs extra. (See Appendix 1 for more information on on-line services.)

On-Line Service Providers

Useful Databases
On-line services have excellent, reliable on-line databases that can be invaluable if you are in business and want to check stock prices, look at market research data, or make flight reservations.

Internet Access
Internet access within the main on-line services has greatly improved over the last year or so. Easy access is now built in to the software provided. In other words, you can launch a Web browser, for instance, simply by clicking the relevant button.

On-Line Charges
Most OSPs charge customers a monthly fee for a set number of hours. There are additional charges for subsequent hours within the billing period. A choice of billing plans is usually available.

POP Coverage
The main OSPs are based in the US and have POP access telephone numbers throughout the world. This can make it easy to stay in touch if you travel frequently.

Shopping Around

Choosing a service provider can be a "chicken and egg" situation for new users. How can I know what I'm going to do on the Internet until I have tried it? How can I try it until I have signed up with a service provider? How do I choose a service provider until I know what I want to do? Fortunately, as these pages show, there are ways of "testing the waters" before you dive into the surf!

WHAT WILL IT COST ME?

Once you start using the Internet regularly, you will soon discover how the prices vary from service to service.

The general pricing trend for Internet service providers is to charge a start-up fee of between $10 and $75 and then a monthly fee of between $12 and $25. These costs (or their equivalent in other countries) are only approximations. New service providers appear every week and some offer what seem to be extremely economical terms. However, as this section of the book shows, cost is only one of your considerations when signing up with a service provider.

The on-line service providers tend to charge in a different way. You rarely need to pay a start-up fee; instead, you are billed a monthly fee of around $6-7 for a fixed number of hours. Subsequent hours (or minutes, in some cases) within the monthly billing period will cost you extra.

On-line service providers usually give you a software starter pack which has everything you need to get connected, to send and receive e-mail, and to browse the Web. However, the software provided by some ISPs may be shareware (see page 47) which you will then need to register for an extra fee.

Internet Access in Your Neighborhood

One way in which you can try out both the Internet service providers and on-line service providers is to visit one of the growing number of public areas that offer Internet access. For a modest hourly or half-hourly fee you can sit at a computer (usually with a fast Internet connection) and surf. You may find such a service in a bookshop, public library, sports center, or educational establishment near you.

Cyberia Café, Paris

Internet Cafés

Internet cafés (or cybercafés, as they are sometimes known) have become very popular in many cities and combine a café atmosphere with a room of computers. Here you are likely to meet people with a wide range of Internet experience – from beginner to expert. If you need help, there should be experts available to tell you how to get started. Once you have spent a few hours in an Internet Café, you will have a far better idea of what the Internet can offer and what sort of service you would use.

Watch the Clock!
If you join a "limited hours" service provider on a trial basis, you may be billed as soon as you exceed the agreed number of free hours. You should contact the service provider before the end of the trial period if you decide not to take out a full subscription to their service.

WHERE TO TRY BEFORE YOU BUY

A good way to assess the different service providers, without committing yourself to an account, is to get hold of a "trial account." When registering some trial accounts, you may need to enter your credit card details, enabling the service provider to bill you automatically if you use the account after the trial period. Other trial accounts simply expire after a specified period. You may also find that some have restricted facilities. For example, you may not be allowed to choose an e-mail name until you register for a full account.

Modem Packages
Some modems come with software offering a free trial account with a service provider. Others may even offer several of these trial accounts.

Call Your Local Service Provider
It does no harm to phone your local service providers and ask whether they can offer you a trial account (see page 31 for a checklist of useful questions to ask when speaking to service providers).

Call Your Friends
Ask any friends with Internet access about their service provider and, if possible, look at the software they are using. Perhaps they will offer you a quick tour of their favorite parts of the Internet as well!

Magazines
Internet magazines can be very useful for finding your local service provider(s) and for comparing performance. They often carry comparison tables that give you an idea of speed of access, reliability, cost, and "downtime" (periods when the service is temporarily unavailable).

Cover CD-ROMs
Check the cover discs given away with computer magazines (especially Internet magazines). You will often find trial accounts offered by various service providers, with full set-up instructions inside the magazine.

Before You Sign Up...

Over the last few pages you will have seen the differences between the types of service that you can receive from service providers. Some companies will provide a connection to the Internet together with a list of telephone access numbers and little more. At the opposite end of the scale, on-line service providers include access to the Internet as just one part of a broader package. Choosing the service provider that's right for you is difficult and will be largely determined by what you consider important. If price is important, an account with an Internet access provider will probably work out to be the cheapest each month. However, for speedy access to well-organized databases of authoritative information, an on-line service provider will rank high.

HOW LONG WILL YOU BE ON-LINE?

Different service providers can and do charge customers in very different ways, which can make it hard to work out which offers the cheapest price. Your choice should be influenced by how much you intend to use the Internet or on-line services. If you are likely to spend more than 15 hours per month on-line, for example, it may be more sensible to choose an Internet service provider that offers unlimited Internet access for a fixed monthly rate. Generally speaking, if you are likely to use the Internet for less than 15 hours, you may prefer to access the Internet via an on-line service, since you will benefit from the extra content that is included in their basic monthly charge.

Access for Travelers
If you travel and want to access your Internet account without needing to make international calls, you should choose a service provider that offers international access numbers. *CompuServe*, for example, has numbers in major cities in many countries. Alternatively, some ISPs make arrangements with local service providers in other countries to act as a "bridge" back to your home.

Internet Software

To access the Internet you need software for dialing the POP access number, and for using FTP, e-mail, and the Web.

❏ Some Internet service providers only give you the most basic software when you sign up with them.

❏ Other ISPs include very good all-in-one packages when you sign up.

❏ Most on-line service providers supply free customized software for accessing their services and the Internet when you sign up. Software for *The Microsoft Network* is included with *Windows 95* (see box on page 27).

Connection Charges

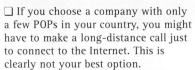

It is very important that you make sure you can dial a local number to connect to your service provider.

❏ If you choose a company with only a few POPs in your country, you might have to make a long-distance call just to connect to the Internet. This is clearly not your best option.

❏ Many large service providers have a wide national network of POP access numbers that are charged at local-rate prices.

❏ Most major on-line service providers offer local telephone access, but these do not all necessarily offer 28,800 bps access (see checklist opposite).

Technical Support

If you are new to the Internet, you will probably need a telephone support line. You might need to use it several times when setting up the Internet software or to get your connection working efficiently (although, of course, this book will help).

❏ The large on-line service providers, such as *AOL* and *CompuServe*, generally provide good backup and telephone support for their customers.

❏ Many small or new ISPs that have grown up overnight have too few staff members to offer effective telephone support. Some only offer support by e-mail, which is not much use if you cannot get your software working!

What Should I Ask?

This checklist covers a few of the main questions you should ask a service provider. You can check off each question as you go. Remember also to ask for a full information pack.

Question	✓	Notes
How Much Will it Cost? • How much is the registration or start-up fee? • Does the monthly fee give unlimited Internet access? *OSPs usually charge a monthly fee for a fixed number of hours, and then make an extra charge for each subsequent hour (or minute).*		
Will I Be Able to Use a Local Telephone Number to Connect to the Internet? In other words: • Where is the POP nearest to my home? *You might also ask how many POPs the company offers, to get some idea of the size of the organization and to know whether you can use the service from other parts of the country at local rate charges.* • Do you offer 28,800 bps access to all your POPs? *You should check this even if you are not using a 28.8K modem, because you will almost certainly want to upgrade a slower modem if you become a regular Web user.*		
Will I Be Able to Use All the Latest Internet Software? • Do you offer a standard PPP connection allowing me to run any TCP/IP Internet application? *If you want to be sure that you can run the latest Internet software, including the latest versions of Web browsers, you should have a standard PPP connection.*		
What Software Do You Provide? • Do you supply: a Web browser? an FTP program? an e-mail program? a newsreader? • Will the software be registered to me or is it shareware? • Does the software automatically install itself? • Do you send it to me or do I have to download it?		
What Support Do You Offer? •What are the opening times of your telephone support lines? • What other support services do you offer?		
What Sort of E-Mail Account Will I Have? • Do you offer POP3 or SMTP e-mail? *POP3 mail is needed for the examples shown in this book.* • What would my e mail address be?		
Which Newsgroups Do You Supply? • Will I be able to access all the Usenet newsgroups? *Some service providers provide only limited access to newsgroups.*		
Can I Put Up My Own Web Pages? • Do you offer free server space for me to put up my own Web pages? If not, what will it cost me?		

Connecting to the Internet

T HE QUALITY OF SOFTWARE SUPPLIED BY INTERNET SERVICE PROVIDERS varies widely. You may be given an integrated suite of Internet programs, comprising a dialer, Web browser, FTP and e-mail programs, and a newsreader. On the other hand, you may simply be given an Internet connection and advised to run your own Internet software, or you may be given shareware that you need to register after a trial period. In this situation, you may prefer to try other Internet programs, such as a different Web browser, for example, before you make that decision. Fortunately, *Windows 95* contains all the software you need to connect to your service provider and get a direct Internet connection. Once you have made the connection, you can run any Internet software, including all the latest shareware that you download. This section gives detailed advice on how to install and configure the *Windows 95* Internet software.

Can I Just Use My Service Provider's Software?
Yes. Some service providers supply excellent software suites that you can augment with your own Internet programs. However, this is not true of all integrated software packages, and you may find it very difficult to run the latest Web browsers, for example. If you set up the *Windows 95* Internet software described in this section, you will be able to bypass this problem.

Using the Windows 95 Internet Software

Windows 95 comes with an essential piece of software called Winsock (see box on this page). Some service providers supply their own version of Winsock that may not always be compatible with the newest Internet programs, although it will work fine with the software they supply you with.

Over the next few pages, you will learn how to install and set up the *Windows 95* software for connecting to the Internet. This procedure can seem quite difficult, since you have to type a lot of complicated-looking settings into a series of dialog boxes. The process is actually quite easy, if you are well prepared, and – on the positive side – you should only need to do it once.

WINDOWS 95 AND MICROSOFT PLUS!
An "Internet Setup Wizard" comes with the optional *Microsoft Plus!* disc or later versions of *Internet Explorer*. It simplifies some of the procedures described on the next few pages. In this book, however, we assume that you are using only the Internet software provided with *Windows 95*.

A GUIDE TO GETTING INSTALLED
Over the next few pages you will connect to your service provider in four easy stages:

Stage One: Installation
How to install the Windows 95 *Internet software (called* Dial-Up Networking*) on your system (if it is not installed already).*

Stage Two: Configuration
How to configure the Dial-Up Networking *software to dial in to your service provider. You will be typing details that relate to your service provider and your Internet account at this stage.*

Stage Three: Creating a Dial-Up Networking Connection
This stage simply creates an icon for quick access to your Internet account. You will need to type the telephone number for your local POP.

Stage Four: Connection
How to dial in using your new Dial-Up Networking icon. What you can expect to see when you have connected to your service provider.

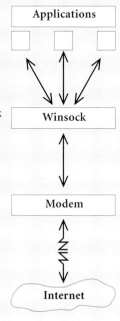

What Is Winsock?

Winsock is short for "Windows Sockets." Basically, Winsock acts as an interface between your PC and the Internet. When you are running any Internet programs (for example, your Web browser or your e-mail program) Winsock translates to the TCP/IP protocol any commands they send, and then transmits the data to your modem and across the Internet. Similarly, data received by your modem is translated from TCP/IP before it is accessed by your Winsock-compliant programs. Winsock manages all the demands made by different Internet programs – even if you have several running at the same time.

Applications

Winsock

Modem

Internet

Gather This Information Before You Turn the Page

Many service providers will give you all the connection information you need with your starter documents. You may also find a document specifically relating to dial-up networking, either with your starter pack, or on the service provider's FTP or Web sites. If you need to check any details, call your service provider; explain that you are setting up Dial-Up Networking in *Windows 95*. It is important that you ask for any other settings that are specific to that service provider. But make sure you don't have these details already. It will leave your service provider's help lines available for more urgent calls, and make a technical support person's day a little easier!

This section is not intended for people using a local area network. You should not attempt to change any network settings without seeking advice from your network administrator.

Dynamic and Static IP Addressing
Most service providers offer "dynamic" IP addressing. This means that you are allocated an IP address by your service provider each time you log on, so it is likely to be different each time. With "static" IP addressing you use the same IP address each time you log on. The following pages show how to connect to the Internet when your provider uses dynamic IP addressing.

Your Dial-Up Checklist

You will need the following information before you can proceed with installation and connection to your service provider. Spend some time gathering all the information mentioned in the checklist below before you follow the steps on the following pages. You will save yourself a lot of time and effort if you have all this information at hand. The checklist below will help you get organized.

• **Your user name**

• **Your password**

• **Your service provider's domain name**
For example, **provider.com**.

• **Your IP address**
An IP address is a unique set of four numbers; for example, 123.243.53.263. You will not need to use your IP address if your service provider offers dynamic IP addressing (see tip box above).

• **The telephone number for your local POP**
This is the number your modem dials to access your service provider.

• **Does your provider support PPP?** `Yes`
Your provider should support PPP. If you have a SLIP account, consult your provider: the steps in this section relate to a PPP account.

• **DNS server**
A Domain Name Server translates IP numbers into names. You may be given IP addresses for more than one DNS server.

• **Dynamic or Static IP address?** `Dynamic` `Static`
The following pages are based on dynamic IP addressing (see tip box above).

• **Does your provider supply a *Windows 95* Dial-Up Networking script?** `Yes` `No`
See page 39.

Although you do not need the following two addresses for Dial-Up Networking, you will need them when you configure e-mail, newsreader, and Web browser software.

• **Name of your provider's news server**

• **Name of your provider's mail server**

Stage One: Installation

The steps on this page show how to install the *Windows 95* Dial-Up Networking software on your computer. You will need to have your *Windows 95* CD or disks on hand. If this software is already installed on your PC, you will find a folder called *Dial-Up Networking* in the *My Computer* folder. In this case, you can move directly to "Stage Two: Configuration" on the next page.

If Dial-Up Networking software is not installed, open the *Control Panel* window, double-click the *Add/Remove Programs* icon, and follow the steps below.

1 In the *Add/Remove Programs Properties* dialog box, click the *Windows Setup* tab, click on *Communications* and then click the *Details* button.

2 In the *Communications* dialog box, check the *Dial-Up Networking* box, then click *OK*. You are now returned to the *Add/Remove Programs Properties* dialog box. Click *OK*.

You will now be prompted to insert your *Windows 95* CD or disks. When the necessary files have been copied to your hard disk, a *Network* warning box will pop up. Click *OK*.

3 In the *Network* dialog box, you need to type entries in the *Computer name* and *Workgroup* boxes. Typing **Default** and **Workgroup** will be sufficient. Click *OK*. (If this dialog box does not appear, simply move to Step 4.)

More files will now be copied to your PC from your *Windows 95* CD or disks.

4 When copying is complete, the *Dial-Up Networking Setup* information box pops up. Read the message, click *OK*, and restart your computer.

5 When your PC restarts, the *Enter Windows Password* dialog box will pop up. (This may not happen if you already use a *Windows* password.) Type a name in the *User name* box and leave the *Password* box blank for now. Click *OK*. The *Set Windows Password* dialog box now appears. Leave both boxes blank and click *OK*.

Installation Complete

You have now installed the Windows 95 *Dial-Up Networking software on your PC.*
You will find the Dial-Up Networking *folder in the* My Computer *folder, a* Start *button shortcut to this folder in the* Accessories *submenu of* Programs, *and an icon called* Network Neighborhood *on your desktop.*

Stage Two: Configuration

With the Dial-Up Networking software installed, you need to configure it by typing settings that relate to your service provider and to your Internet account. For this stage, it is very important that you use the information supplied by your service provider. All the information you need for this section is referred to in the checklist on page 31.

Before you begin, open the *Control Panel* window, and double-click the *Network* icon. Then follow these steps:

1 In the *Network* dialog box, click the *Configuration* tab, then click *Add*.

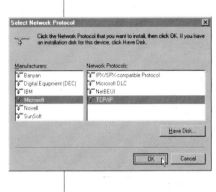

2 In the *Select Network Component Type* dialog box, select *Protocol* and then click *Add*.

3 In the *Select Network Protocol* dialog box, select *Microsoft* in the *Manufacturers* panel, and *TCP/IP* in the *Network Protocols* panel. Then click *OK*. You now return to the *Network* dialog box. Click *OK*.

More files will now be copied from your *Windows 95* CD or disks.

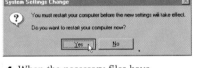

4 When the necessary files have been copied to your hard disk, the *Systems Settings Change* query box will pop up. Click *Yes* to restart your computer.

5 When your PC has restarted, return to the *Control Panel* window and double-click the *Network* icon. On the *Configuration* page of the *Network* dialog box click *IPX/SPX-compatible Protocol* and click *Remove*. Then click *NetBEUI*, and click *Remove* again. (These components are not required for your Internet connection.)

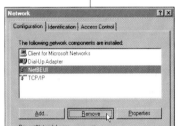

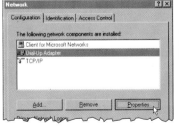

6 Now click *Dial-Up Adapter* and then *Properties*. The *Dial-Up Adapter Properties* dialog box will appear.

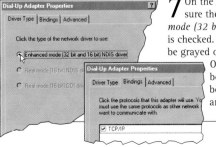

7 On the *Driver Type* page, make sure the button next to *Enhanced mode (32 bit and 16 bit) NDIS driver* is checked. The other options should be grayed out. Click the *Bindings* tab. On the *Bindings* page, the box next to *TCP/IP* should be checked. Finally, click *OK* and continue to Step 8.

8 On the *Configuration* page of the *Network* dialog box, click *TCP/IP*, then *Properties*.

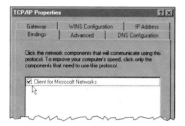

9 In the *TCP/IP Properties* dialog box, click the *Bindings* tab. On the *Bindings* page, the box next to *Client for Microsoft Networks* should be checked. Now click the *IP Address* tab.

10 On the *IP Address* page, check the *Obtain an IP address automatically* box and click *OK*. Then click *OK* in the *Network* dialog box.

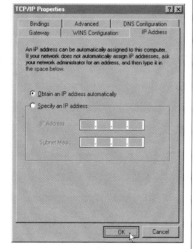

11 The *Systems Settings Change* query box pops up again. Click *Yes* to restart your PC.

Configuration Complete

The Dial-Up Networking software is now configured on your PC. You are ready to create a Dial-Up Networking connection that will give you access to your service provider.

Stage Three: Creating a Dial-Up Networking Connection

You are now ready to create a Dial-Up Networking connection for accessing your service provider. In Stage Three, you will be typing settings that relate to your modem, your telephone access (or POP) number for your service provider, and your TCP/IP settings. It is important that you follow precisely any instructions supplied by your service provider, making any necessary changes in the steps below.

To begin, click the *Start* button, choose *Programs*, and then *Dial-Up Networking* from the *Accessories* menu.

1 In the *Welcome to Dial-Up Networking* box that pops up, click *Next*. (If this box does not appear, double-click the *Make New Connection* icon in the Dial-Up Networking window.) The *Make New Connection* dialog box appears.

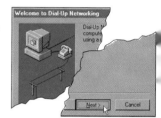

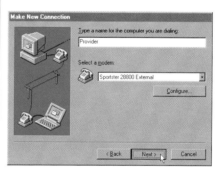

2 In the box below *Type a name for the computer you are dialing*, type the name of your service provider ("Provider" in this example). Then click *Next*.

3 In the window that appears, type the telephone area code and number of your service provider in the appropriate boxes. Change the setting in the *Country code* box, if necessary, by clicking the arrow on the right of the box and choosing from the drop-down menu. Click *Next*. Finally, click *Finish* in the dialog box that appears.

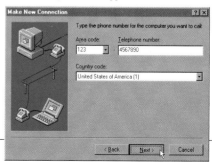

4 A new icon (called *Provider* in this example) will now appear in the *Dial-Up Networking* window. Right-click this icon and choose *Properties* from the drop-down menu.

5 In the *Provider* dialog box (the box will have the same name that you typed in Step 2), click the *Configure* button. The *Properties* box for your modem will appear.

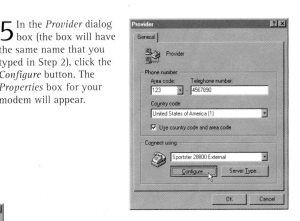

6 In your modem's *Properties* dialog box, click the *Options* tab. Then check the box next to *Bring up terminal window after dialing*, and click *OK*. You are returned to the *Provider* dialog box.

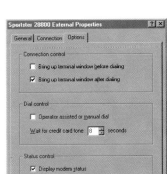
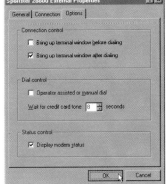
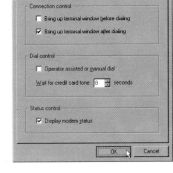

7 In the *Provider* dialog box, click *Server Type*.

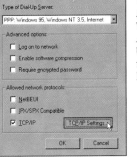

8 In the *Server Types* dialog box, ensure that the entry in the *Type of Dial-Up Server* box reads "PPP; Windows 95, Windows NT 3.5, Internet." Under *Advanced options*, uncheck all the boxes. Under *Allowed network protocols* ensure that only the *TCP/IP* box is checked. Finally, click the *TCP/IP Settings* button.

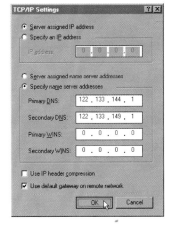

9 In the *TCP/IP Settings* dialog box, check the box next to *Specify name server addresses*. Type the DNS server address or addresses, as supplied by your service provider, in the appropriate boxes. Click *OK*. Finally, click *OK* in the *Server types* box, and then click *OK* in the *Provider* dialog box.

Creating a Dial-Up Networking Connection Complete

You are finally ready to connect to your service provider using your new Dial-Up Networking settings. The settings you have typed in this stage are only valid for this particular Dial-Up Networking connection. If you use more than one service provider, you can set up another Dial-Up Networking connection with settings relevant to that service provider.

Stage Four: Connection

Finally, you are ready to connect to your service provider using the Dial-Up Networking connection you created in Stage Three. During the login process you will need to type a few simple details. The exact sequence and appearance of this login process varies between service providers, but you will usually be asked for:

❑ your user name or login name

❑ your password

❑ the protocol (ie, PPP)

Follow the steps below to connect to the Internet.

1 In the *Dial-Up Networking* folder, double-click the icon for the Dial-Up Networking connection you created in Stage Three (in this example, the *Provider* icon).

Dialing Other Service Providers
The settings you typed in Stage Three are only valid for this particular Dial-Up Networking connection. If you use more than one service provider, you can set up another Dial-Up Networking connection with settings relevant to that service provider.

2 In the *Connect To* dialog box, type your information in the *User name* and *Password* boxes, then click *Connect*.

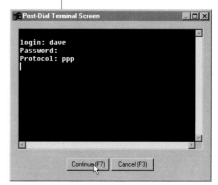

3 In the *Post-Dial Terminal Screen* window, type any details required by your service provider when prompted and press the Return key each time. In this example you are asked for your login name and your password. If you are prompted for "protocol," type **ppp**. Some information from your service provider may appear. Click *Continue* to proceed.

CONNECTED!

4 The *Connected To Provider* box appears when you have successfully connected. You can now launch your Internet programs.

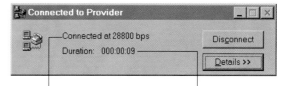

Connected at...
Even if you have a 28.8K modem, you may not see "Connected at 28800 bps." The speed shown here depends on how your modem is configured and shows either the speed at which your modem is communicating with your PC, or your service provider's modem (known as the DTE speed and DCE speed respectively). Therefore, other speeds, such as 14400 bps or 115200 bps, may be shown.

Duration
This displays the amount of time that you have been connected to your provider, shown in hours, minutes, and seconds.

Connection Complete

You can now run any of your Internet applications; e.g., a Web browser, FTP program, or newsreader.
To disconnect from your service provider, click the Disconnect *button in the* Connected To Provider *window.*

Dial-Up Scripting

Use a Sample Script

Many service providers will supply preconfigured scripts, leaving you to type your password and user name in the appropriate lines. If you can use a dummy script from your service provider, it will save you a lot of time and effort. Microsoft provides a sample script called **PPPmenu.scp** when you install the Dial-Up Scripting Tool. Look for it in the *Accessories* folder of the *Program Files* folder.

It is possible to automate the login process described in Stage Four (opposite) by using Microsoft's Dial-Up Scripting Tool. Before you use this software, you need to write a script. This script is a text file, containing a set of commands that instruct your computer to wait for a query from your service provider and then transmit the details you have specified. You use the Dial-Up Scripting Tool to assign a script to a particular Dial-Up Networking connection (see "Assigning Your Script" below). For example, if you assign a script to the Provider Dial-Up Networking connection, you simply bypass Step 3 in Stage Four.

Using Dial-Up Scripting is not necessarily the next "stage" in connecting to the Internet. You have already done all the hard work in Stage Three. Dial-Up Scripting simply makes logging on a little tidier (see "Where to Find the Windows 95 Dial-Up Scripting Tool" below).

Notes for the User
Every line preceded by a semi-colon in this script is not used during login. This text is included for reference when you are editing the script.

Send Your User Name
This sequence waits for the prompt "login" from your service provider. It then transmits your login name. "$USERID" reads the information that you typed at Step 2, Stage Four.

```
provider - Notepad
File  Edit  Search  Help

;
; sample script file to automate login to PROVIDER CON
;
proc main

waitfor "login"
transmit $USERID
transmit "^M"
waitfor "password"
transmit $PASSWORD
transmit "^M"
waitfor "protocol"
transmit "PPP"
transmit "^M"

endproc
```

Send a Return
The "^M" command in this script sends an instruction that is equivalent to pressing the Return key.

Send the Protocol
This sequence waits for the prompt "protocol" and then sends the letters "PPP."

Send Your Password
This sequence waits for the prompt "password," then transmits your password. "$PASSWORD" is similar to the "$USERID" in that it reads the information you type in the Connect to dialog box.

Where to Find the Windows 95 Dial-Up Scripting Tool

• On your *Windows 95* CD. To install it, use the *Add/Remove Programs Properties* dialog box, click the *Windows Setup* tab and then the *Have Disk* button. Navigate to the *admin\apptools\dscript* folder, click *rnaplus* in the left-hand panel, and then click *OK*. (After you have restarted your PC, a *Start* menu entry for *Dial-Up Scripting Tool* will appear in the *Accessories* sub-menu for *Programs*.)

Unfortunately, the floppy disk version of *Windows 95* does not contain this utility, but it is also available from the following sources:

❏ The *Microsoft Plus!* CD

❏ The Microsoft FTP site at **ftp.microsoft.com**

ASSIGNING YOUR SCRIPT

When you have completed your dial-up script, you use the Dial-Up Scripting Tool to associate it with the Dial-Up Networking connection you created in Stage Three. To do this, click *Provider* (in this example) in the *Connections* panel, then click the *Browse* button. Navigate to your script file (in this example **provider.scp**). Then click *Close*. By checking the box next to *Step through script*, you can monitor each stage of the login process. This can be useful if troubleshooting is necessary.

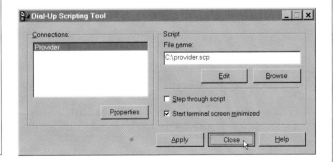

Chapter 2

Downloading Files and Sending E-Mail

The ability to transfer information rapidly across the globe, at the click of a mouse button, makes the Internet an incredible and unique resource. Chapter 2 introduces two of the most common ways to move information across the Net – File Transfer Protocol (FTP) and electronic mail. FTP sites around the world contain a vast range of files. This chapter explains how you can log on to these sites and transfer files – including programs, utilities, games, and graphics – to your PC. It also describes how to send and receive e-mail messages, and how to use e-mail to perform a wide range of other Internet activities.

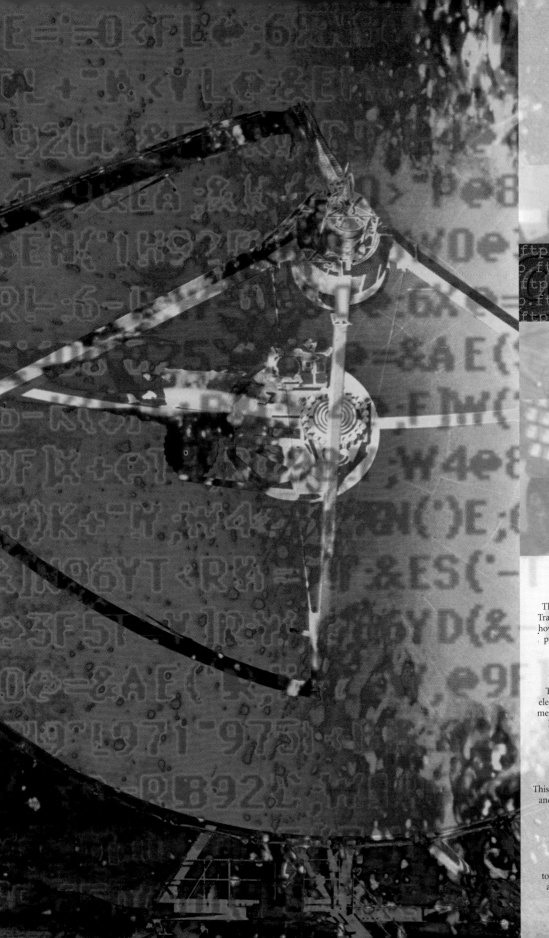

2

Transferring Files with FTP

ACROSS THE INTERNET THERE ARE MILLIONS OF FILES AND PROGRAMS available for you to try out, for free. Using a process called File Transfer Protocol (FTP), you can retrieve any such file from a distant computer and transfer it to your hard disk (a process called downloading a file). The protocol part of FTP refers to the series of standard, predefined messages that allow a file to be retrieved regardless of the type of computer you are using.

Downloading Files

To transfer files using FTP, you need to have a file transfer program (known as an FTP client) installed on your hard disk. There are many such programs available for just about every type of computer system. When you sign up with an Internet service provider, one of the items it should supply is an FTP program for downloading files. If it does not, you can find shareware programs on many CD-ROMs included free with computer magazines. You can also download files to your computer by using the transfer features of the main Web browsers, such as *Netscape Navigator* and Microsoft's *Internet Explorer.*

FROM THE INTERNET TO YOUR PC
You might see some complex descriptions about how FTP actually works, but in essence it is very straightforward. The software on your PC is called the FTP client and the remote computer you are contacting is called the FTP server or host.

Sounds
Words, music, and noises of all descriptions are available from FTP sites. For example, visit **ftp.cc.umanitoba.ca** *to find a collection of sound clips from the Star Trek TV series.*

TRANSFERRING FILES FROM AN FTP SITE
There are many ways of logging on to FTP sites and transferring files. The two most usual are to use an FTP client program, such as *CuteFTP* (see page 44), or a Web browser. In the *Netscape Navigator* Web browser, for example, you can access an FTP site by changing the URL (site address) from **http://** to **ftp://** and typing the site's address.

FTP via a Web Browser

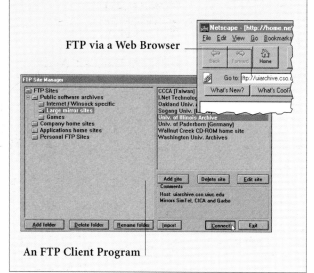

An FTP Client Program

ANONYMOUS FTP
"Anonymous FTP" is one of the common jargon terms you will find when exploring the Internet. It simply describes the way you access computers that contain files for public access. Each time you want to transfer a file from a remote site, you actually need to log on to that computer to view the files stored on its hard disk. This would become increasingly difficult if you had to remember a different user name and password for each of the thousands of remote computers that you might want to log on to and explore.

To get around this problem, almost all FTP sites have a special user account with only one user name, and it can be accessed by anybody. When asked for your user name, all you do is type **anonymous**; for the password you normally type your e-mail address. Not all remote servers will check that you have entered your real e-mail address, but some will. It is considered polite and good "netiquette" always to use your correct e-mail address as the password.

Software

Almost any type of software is available for you to try or even use indefinitely. For example, you can download many Windows 95 drivers and updates from **ftp.microsoft.com**.

Documents

There is more information on the Internet for you to download than can be safely guessed at. For example, the Gutenberg Project archive (at **uiarchive.cso.uiuc.edu/ pub/etext/gutenberg***) holds thousands of complete electronic texts from Aesop's Fables to Zen and the Art of the Internet.*

Images

Photographs, video and animation clips, illustrations, stills from movies – almost any type of image you can think of is available on an FTP site. For example, there is a huge collection of NASA space photographs at **explorer.arc.nasa.gov/pub/SPACE**.

How Do I Know Where to Look?

As with everything else on the Net, one of the biggest problems with FTP is finding out what is actually out there, and where to find it. If you want to keep your printer busy for a long time, you could download and print a full list of FTP sites. This can run to many hundreds of pages! A more sensible approach is to use a database of FTP sites called Archie. You can access Archie via the Web at **http://archie.internic.net** but this is only one of dozens of Archie servers around the world. If you know the name of a program or file that you want to locate, you can type it in, and Archie will give you the address of the FTP site or sites where it is held. Alternatively, you can query the database using keywords to find out which FTP sites hold information related to particular subjects. (See page 55 for how to query Archie using e-mail.) You can also access Archie using dedicated client software, such as *WSArchie*.

Web Search

An Archie search using Netscape Navigator.

WSArchie

A popular client program, used for accessing Archie databases.

Logging on to an FTP Site

To access an FTP site and transfer files from it to your
hard disk, you need an FTP program or a Web browser that
supports FTP. Your service provider has probably supplied
you with an FTP program, but there are many alternatives
available on the Internet if you care to experiment. Some
dedicated FTP programs are packed with features; others
offer a simple command-line interface. These pages feature
a shareware program called *CuteFTP*, developed by Alex
Kunadze. This program is available from many Internet sites.

TRANSFERRING FILES WITH CUTEFTP

CuteFTP requires no additional configuration after you have
installed it on your PC. The program's *FTP Site Manager*
provides addresses for a large number of sites, arranged by
category, as well as the option to add your own favorites.
The steps on these pages show how to connect to Microsoft's
FTP site and download a copy of the *Windows 95* newsletter.

1 Double-click the *Cuteftp*
icon in the *CuteFTP* folder.
The program's main window
and the *FTP Site Manager*
window will open.

2 In the *FTP Site Manager*
window, click *Personal
FTP Sites* in the left-hand
panel. Then click the *Add
site* button.

3 Type a word or phrase in
the *Site Label* box to identify
the site you wish to access.
Type the site's address in the
Host Address box and include additional directory
information in the *Initial Remote Directory* box.
Type **/Peropsys/Win_News/News&Events/WinNews**
in this example.

4 Check the boxes next to
Anonymous in the *Login type*
panel and *Auto-Detect* in the
Transfer type panel. (Some sites
require you to type your e-mail
address in the *Password* box).
Finally, click *OK*.

5 The name you typed in the *Site
Label* box in Step 3 will now
appear in the right-hand panel of
the *FTP Site Manager* dialog box.
Click on this name to highlight it
and then click *Connect*.

Other Popular FTP Programs

☐ **WS-FTP32**

Freeware. This program is easy for beginners to use.
More information is available at its home page on
the Web at: **http://www.csra.net/junodj/ws_ftp32.htm**.

☐ **FTP Explorer**

This is currently free for noncommercial use.
Its interface is similar to that of *Windows Explorer*.

You can find both clients and more at the following
Web page: **http://www.windows95.com/apps/ftp.html**.

6 Read the welcome messages or announcements that appear. Click *OK* to proceed.

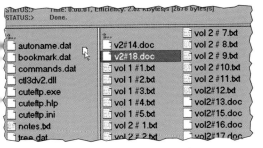

7 When you have successfully logged on, a directory list for the remote site will appear in the right-hand panel of the main *CuteFTP* window. (See page 46 for how to navigate around sites.) To transfer a file from the FTP site to your hard disk, simply click on the appropriate file in the right-hand panel and drag it over the left-hand panel.

8 The *Confirm* dialog box will appear. Click *Yes* to continue. When the file is successfully transferred, its name will appear in the left-hand panel of the main window.

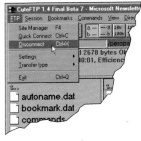

9 To disconnect from a site, choose *Disconnect* from the *FTP* menu in the main window.

Windows 95's FTP Program
There is an FTP program supplied with *Windows 95*, although it is not as user-friendly as the examples referred to on these pages. It provides a simple command-line interface where you type UNIX-style commands. If you prefer working with a graphical interface, this program is probably best avoided. To run it, choose *Run* from the *Start* menu and type **ftp**.

Connecting with Other FTP Programs

In principle, you follow the same procedure in all FTP programs to log on to an FTP site. You need to type the following information:

❏ **The Site Address**
The site address can include information about the directories on that site. For example, **ftp.microsoft.com** is the main site address for Microsoft's FTP server. The full address for the directory containing the *Windows 95* newsletter is **ftp.microsoft.com/Peropsys/ Win_News/News&Events/WinNews**. You can use the full address if you happen to know it, and if your FTP program lets you type these extra directories (see Step 3 on page 44). Otherwise, use the main site address and navigate to the directory you require from within your FTP program. The / symbol indicates subfolders within the main folder or site.

❏ **The User Name**
Type **anonymous** where a user name is required.

❏ **The Password**
Type your e-mail address as a password.

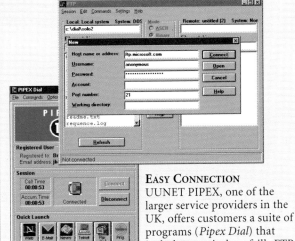

EASY CONNECTION
UUNET PIPEX, one of the larger service providers in the UK, offers customers a suite of programs (*Pipex Dial*) that includes a typical no-frills FTP program. When you click the *FTP* button, the *New* dialog box (above) pops up. Users then supply the information described on the right.

FTP Button
The main Pipex Dial *window showing the quick start* FTP *button.*

Navigating an FTP Site

Once you have logged on to an FTP site, you will often need to navigate through the directories and subdirectories to locate the file you are looking for. (In *Windows 95*, directories are usually known as folders.)

Sometimes, if you try to log on directly to a specific subdirectory on a site (see Step 3 on page 44) you may find yourself in the server's default directory. A common reason for this is that the FTP server has been reorganized, and the subdirectory you are trying to access has been moved, renamed, or deleted. If this happens, you will need to navigate around the site to search for the file you want, as described on this page.

You may simply want to explore the contents of a site. In either case, you should read any "help," "readme," or "index" files on the server before exploring further.

HOW TO MOVE AROUND AN FTP SITE

The illustration below shows how to use *CuteFTP* to access directories and files on an FTP site, but most FTP programs share the same main features. If you haven't read the help file supplied with a new shareware program, it is advisable to use the program's menu commands when accessing an FTP site. This is because certain *Windows 95* options, such as double-clicking a file to open it, may not work in quite the same way in other programs. In some FTP programs, for example, double-clicking a text file will transfer it to your hard disk rather than open it for browsing.

Virus Alert!
There is always a danger, when you transfer files over the Internet, that you may be downloading one infected with a virus. Although this happens infrequently, you can take steps to prevent it by using an antivirus program to scan any downloaded program files before you use them. Many powerful freeware and shareware antivirus tools are available from Internet sites.

Viewing Text Files
To view a text file, such as an "index" or "readme" file, highlight the file and choose View *from the* Commands *menu.*

Directory Information
These boxes show the active directories. Here, the download directory is open on the hard disk, and the root directory is open on the FTP server. If you double-click the peropsys *folder in the panel below, the right-hand box will change to* /peropsys*.*

Status Box
The status box gives you information about the status of your FTP session – for example, the progress of file transfer.

Moving Up a Directory
To move to a higher directory, double-click this symbol. It does not appear when you are in the top-level, or root, directory of the server.

Hard Disk Panel
The left-hand panel relates to your hard disk. In this example, a folder called download *is being used on the hard disk for saving files transferred from the Internet.*

FTP Server Panel
The right-hand panel relates to the FTP server. Navigate to the folder from which you intend to transfer files to your hard disk.

Moving Down a Directory
To view the contents of a directory, double-click a folder icon in the right-hand panel.

CuteFTP 1.4 Final Beta 7 - Microsoft (ftp.microsoft.com)

FTP Session Bookmarks Commands View Directory Window Help

c:\download

STATUS:> Time: 0:00:01, Efficiency: 0.56 KBytes/s [577 bytes/s]
226 Transfer complete.
STATUS:> Successfully received index.txt

bussys	0	01/05/96 23:32
deskapps	0	09/08/95 0:00
developr	0	27/10/95 0:00
KBHelp	0	10/02/96 1:36
MSCorp	0	20/10/95 0:00
msdownload	0	07/06/96 2:47
peropsys	0	11/10/95 0:00
Products	0	30/11/95 0:00
Services	0	08/05/96 18:38
Softlib	0	30/05/96 1:39
solutions	0	08/04/96 14:21
dirmap.htm	7,905	05/10/95 0:00
disclaimer.txt	712	25/08/94 0:00 self explanatory
index.txt	577	15/01/96 18:15 this file
ls-IR.txt	7,642,822	07/06/96 11:07
ls-IR.Z	977,227	07/06/96 11:08
LS-LR.ZIP	819,521	07/06/96 11:08 complete listing of all file

What Is "Free" Software?

The software that you can transfer to your hard disk from the Internet is likely to be either "shareware," "freeware," or "public domain." Some of these types of software carry conditions that you are legally obliged to comply with, so it is important to check the conditions that apply to any file you download from an FTP site. Most software programs distributed via the Net will include a text file giving you all the information you need to know about the author, the license, and any action that you may be required to take.

Shareware

❑ *Free to download.*

❑ *Free to try for a limited period.*

❑ *You must register the software after the trial period and pay a fee, or stop using it.*

❑ *Protected by copyright.*

You may also see "postcardware" and "nagware" (both are forms of shareware). One requires you to send your registration on a picture postcard; the other constantly reminds you if you haven't registered yet.

Public Domain

❑ *Free to download and use.*

❑ *Free from copyright protection.*

❑ *May be altered and used for profit.*

❑ *Must be explicitly declared as public domain by the author. If it is not, you should assume that copyright applies.*

Freeware

❑ *Free to download and use.*

❑ *You do not need to register it.*

❑ *Protected by copyright.*

Why Register Shareware?

❑ You usually get added benefits. The registered version of *CuteFTP*, for example, will give you extra features not included in the shareware version. This includes technical support by e-mail and free upgrades in the future.

❑ Your registration fee allows the author to fund further product development.

❑ Shareware authors usually spend next to nothing on advertising and promotion. This means that they are able to license their software to you more cheaply than other developers. It is argued that if people refuse to register shareware, the widespread availability of cheap, quality software will gradually decline.

Common File Types

When you visit FTP sites you'll see all kinds of files with different extensions. These usually tell you at a glance what type of information a file contains. Some of these files may be compressed or encoded and will require special applications to "unlock" them (see Appendix 3).

Video
Common video file formats are avi, mov, dl, gr, mpg.

Images
Common image file extensions are jpg, gif, tif, bmp, pcd.

Audio
Common audio file formats are wav, mid, voc, au.

Programs
Common extensions for application programs are com, exe, bat.

Compressed Files
Some of the extensions used for compressed files are zip, lzh, gz, z, zoo, arj.

Text
Common text file formats are txt, doc, ps, eps, htm, html.

Only Download Files Your Computer Can Handle
Not all the files available at FTP sites will be compatible with your computer. For example, it is useless to download a Macintosh file if you have a PC, or a movie if you don't have a player to view it on. Some files may even require special hardware to get the best results. MPEG video, for example, runs much faster with an MPEG card.

Electronic Mail

For many people, one of the most important reasons for getting connected to the Internet is the capability to send and receive electronic mail (e-mail). With e-mail you can send messages to any other person who has an Internet account. You can even include other files, such as images and spreadsheet files, with your message. Best of all, your message can arrive at its destination within minutes of your sending it. Your incoming e-mail messages are stored in your own mailbox on your service provider's mail server, waiting for you to "collect" them the next time you connect to the Internet.

Why Use E-Mail?

E-mail is everywhere! Once you start looking, you'll discover that most businesses now have an electronic mailing address together with the more "old-fashioned" telephone and fax numbers. An electronic mail message might be just a few lines of text (asking a friend to join you for lunch, for example) or you can send much larger documents. It is much more convenient and economical to send a message or document by e-mail than by conventional mail or fax. E-mail is also delivered much faster than conventional mail.

There are dozens of programs that can manage all your electronic mail messages for you. With an Internet account, you can send e-mail from within many applications, such as word processing programs or Web browsers. Internet "add-ons" that include e-mail features are now available for many widely used programs, such as *Microsoft Word*.

HOW PRIVATE IS ELECTRONIC MAIL?

E-mail is possibly less private than conventional mail since its contents could be read by anyone who has access to the recipient's computer; therefore, it is wise to be cautious about sending sensitive information via e-mail unless you have some way of protecting the contents (by using "encryption" software, for example).

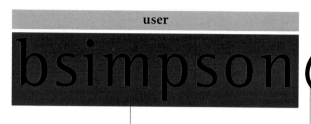

user

Your Name
The first part of your e-mail address is your user name. You can choose any user name, as long as that name has not already been registered by another subscriber. You could use your full name, first name, or an alias. Some service providers allocate numbers instead of, or as an alternative to, user names.

The @ Symbol
The @ (at) symbol separates your user name from the domain name of your address.

THE WAY E-MAIL WORKS

It must be remembered that although e-mail is much faster than conventional mail – which Internet buffs call "snail mail" – it is often only as reliable as the person collecting it. If the recipient forgets to check his or her mail for weeks, the advantages of fast delivery are negated.

Finding E-Mail Addresses

If you are unsure of the address of a person or an organization you want to contact, the following Web sites are a good place to start looking. They have thousands of addresses listed and you can search their databases using keywords.

http://www.whowhere.com
http://okra.ucr.edu/okra
http://www.four11.com

1 Type your message using a suitable e-mail program.

2 Once you have addressed and sent your e-mail, it gets encoded by a modem and sent down the phone line as an analog signal.

YOUR ADDRESS EXPLAINED

Everyone who is connected to the Internet has a unique mailing address. An e-mail address looks unlike any other kind of address. It has two main parts: the user name and the domain name. These are separated by an @ symbol. The number of individual domains in your address "domain name" is determined by the number of branches required to sort mail logically at your mail site. Some addresses have as many as five or six domains, others only have two. If anyone gives you an e-mail address you should type it exactly as you are given it. Although addresses are usually lower case, some mail systems are case-sensitive.

Type of Organization
This domain identifies your provider's type of organization, which may vary according to country. For example, .com is a commercial company in the US; .co is its UK equivalent. In the US, .edu is an educational establishment; it is .ac in the UK.

domains

provider.com

Country Code
If your provider is based outside the US your address will have an additional domain for the country, represented by a unique two-letter code. For example .co.uk is a UK-based commercial company; .or.jp is an organization based in Japan.

.co.uk

Your Provider
The name of your Internet service provider (the company that gives you Internet access). A provider is responsible for sending and receiving messages to and from individual users.

The ● Symbol
Periods or dots separate the various domains of your address. An e-mail address does not include any spaces.

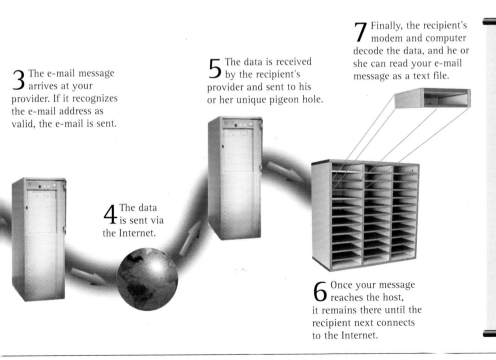

3 The e-mail message arrives at your provider. If it recognizes the e-mail address as valid, the e-mail is sent.

4 The data is sent via the Internet.

5 The data is received by the recipient's provider and sent to his or her unique pigeon hole.

6 Once your message reaches the host, it remains there until the recipient next connects to the Internet.

7 Finally, the recipient's modem and computer decode the data, and he or she can read your e-mail message as a text file.

What Happens if I Get the Address Wrong?
As with the normal postal delivery system, your electronic mail messages need to be correctly addressed. If the computer trying to deliver your message does not recognize the mailing address, it will automatically send you a warning e-mail. You'll see this message the next time you look in your mailbox or, sometimes, days later. In some systems, especially the on-line services, you can generate a receipt when your e-mail has been correctly delivered and read by the recipient.

Using an E-Mail Program

THERE ARE MANY DIFFERENT WAYS IN WHICH YOU CAN SEND AND RECEIVE electronic mail using your PC. Many users, especially those whose on-line activity is centered around the World Wide Web, use the e-mail facilities in Web browsers such as *Netscape Navigator* (see page 65). There are also many dedicated e-mail programs, of which Qualcomm's *Eudora* is probably the most widely used. *Eudora Pro* is the commercial version of the program, but you can download a freeware version (called *Eudora Light*) from many Internet sites. *Eudora Light* is available from Qualcomm's FTP site at **ftp.qualcomm.com**.

Setting Up Eudora

To use *Eudora* you must have a POP3 account. This is a specific type of e-mail protocol used by the vast majority of service providers. If you have any doubts about the type of e-mail account you have, you should check with your service provider.

When you first run the program you will be asked to provide some configuration details. You will need to know your e-mail address and the name of your service provider's mail server. When you are ready, open the folder in which you have installed *Eudora* and follow the steps below.

1 Double-click the *Eudora* icon. The *Settings* dialog box pops up with *Getting Started* highlighted in the *Category* panel.

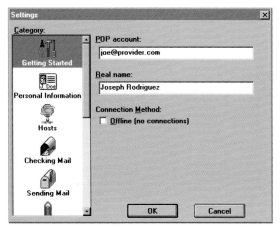

2 In the *POP account* box, type your e-mail address. Type your name in the *Real name* box.

3 Click on *Hosts* in the *Category* panel. The *POP account* box will contain the entry you made in the previous step. Type the name of your service provider's mail server (see page 33) in the *SMTP* box. Finally, click *OK* to complete the basic configuration.

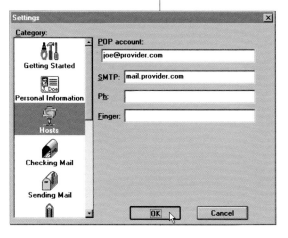

SENDING A MESSAGE WITH EUDORA

Sending a message using *Eudora* is an extremely simple process. Once you have configured the basic program settings all you need to know is the e-mail address of the person you want to contact. It is possible to write an e-mail off-line and then send it from *Eudora* when you next connect to the Internet (see tip box on opposite page). This example shows how to send an e-mail while you are on-line. First make your Internet connection, launch *Eudora*, then follow these steps.

1 Click the *New Message* button. A window called *No Recipient, No Subject* will appear. Your own name and e-mail address will already be displayed.

2 Place the cursor alongside "To." Type the e-mail address of the recipient. In general, this will be in lower-case letters. Press the Tab key. This will move the cursor alongside "Subject."

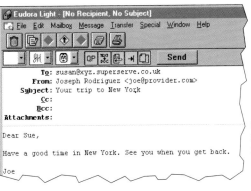

3 Type a brief description of the subject of the e-mail. Press the Tab key again three times. You can now type your message.

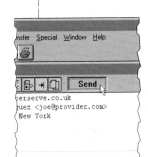

4 When you are ready to send your message, click the *Send* button.

Helpful Descriptions
Get into the habit of entering meaningful subject descriptions for your messages, especially if you are posting to a mailing list (see page 54). This gives the recipients the option of deciding whether your communication is of urgent interest to them.

Attaching a Document

You can use many e-mail programs to send files from your hard disk by "attaching" them to your message. For example, if you want to attach a document to an e-mail message using *Eudora*, choose *Attach File* from the *Message* menu before you click the *Send* button. (You would do this after Step 3 and before Step 4 above.) This will open the *Attach File* dialog box, allowing you to navigate your hard disk until you find the document you want to attach. Incompatibilities can occur between e-mail programs. If the recipient can't view an attachment you have sent, ask which encoding method his or her e-mail program supports. This will usually be MIME or UUEncode (or BINHEX for Apple Macintosh users). If you intend to send large files you can save time and money by using a compression program to reduce the overall size (see Appendix 3).

Receiving Mail with Eudora

Eudora can inform you automatically each time a new piece of mail arrives while you are connected to the Internet. How it does this depends on the options you set up. Choose *Settings* from the *Special* menu, and then *Getting Attention* from the *Category* panel. You will see three options. Click the check boxes to activate the ones you want. The first option displays a dialog box to alert you to incoming messages. The second option automatically opens the mailbox and displays your message. The third option plays a sound each time a new message appears.

OPENING THE MAILBOX MANUALLY

If you do not want to be alerted when you receive new messages, you can manually open the mailbox using the *In* window. The e-mails listed in the *In* window stay there until you decide to delete them. They can also be organized so that your mail is sorted by name or date. The steps below show you how to open the mailbox manually.

Microsoft Exchange
Windows 95 comes with its own e-mail program called *Microsoft Exchange*. If you subscribe to more than one service provider, this program can be set up to handle e-mail from all your accounts. For further information, double-click the *Inbox* icon on your desktop, and access *Microsoft Exchange Help Topics* from the *Help* menu. You may first need to install *Microsoft Exchange* using the *Add/Remove Programs* utility in the *Windows 95* Control Panel.

1 To read incoming e-mails, choose *In* from the *Mailbox* menu. The *In* window appears.

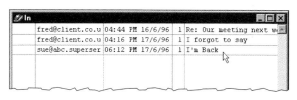

2 The *In* window contains details of all e-mails sent to your address. To read a message double-click anywhere on the line.

3 The message appears in a new window. The window's title bar will contain your e-mail address and the subject line of the message.

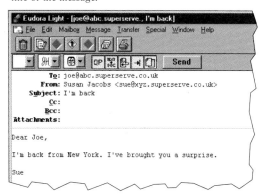

Other Popular E-Mail Programs

❑ **Pegasus Mail**

Freeware. This program is available from the Pegasus home page at **http://www.pegasus.usa.com** on the Web. *Pegasus Mail* add-ons and software support are also available from this site.

❑ **ConnectSoft E-Mail Connection**

Freeware. This feature-laden Internet-only program is available from the following site:

http://www.connectsoft.com/corp/products/download.html

Time-Saving Tips

Sooner or later, you will build up a large list of e-mail contacts. Each time you want to send someone an e-mail, it can be tiresome having to look up and type the address. Most e-mail programs make life easier by providing an address book that stores and manages your list of e-mail addresses. *Eudora*'s address book allows you to store e-mail addresses and select them from a drop-down menu when you want to send a new message. The following steps describe how to add an address to your address book.

1 To save an e-mail address when composing a message, highlight the outgoing address by holding down the mouse button and dragging across the full e-mail address.

2 Choose *Add as Recipient* from the *Special* menu and release the mouse button. The address is now stored.

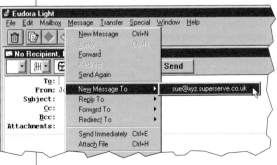

3 This address now appears when you choose *New Message To* from the *Message* menu. When you choose an address from the drop-down menu that appears, a new message window appears. You can now type the text of your message.

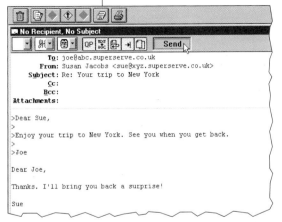

REPLYING TO AN E-MAIL

A high proportion of the e-mails circulating around the Internet are direct responses to other e-mails. When you want to reply to a message, you can save yourself time by using *Eudora*'s "Reply" command. When you are reading a piece of mail, choose *Reply* from the *Message* menu. This produces a new message, with the original contents highlighted and indented with brackets. This is especially useful if you are carrying out a long-running "conversation" over a number of e-mails. In such cases it's a good idea, when responding to a specific point, to keep the original text in your reply. The recipient will be able to tell your response apart from his or her original mail because of the brackets.

The Internet by Electronic Mail

E LECTRONIC MAIL IS FAR MORE FLEXIBLE AND POWERFUL than you might at first imagine. As well as sending messages to other people on the Internet, you can also use e-mail to run a program (such as a "search" program) on a remote computer, and have the results of your query sent back to you. Electronic mail also offers a great way to stay in touch with special interest groups. All you need to do is send a simple "subscribe" message and you will receive automatic updates from a mailing list of correspondents by e-mail.

Mailing Lists

One of the more powerful tasks you can perform with electronic mail is to join a mailing list (a database of people who have an interest in a particular subject). After you have subscribed to a mailing list, you will receive regular information by e-mail about the subject that particular list is concerned with. These e-mails are automatically delivered to you by a "listserver" (see tip box), which sends you e-mail until you choose to unsubscribe. Mailing lists provide a way of keeping up with developments in a particular field of interest at minimum effort and on-line cost. They also allow you to share your own knowledge with anyone else interested enough to join the same list. With thousands of different lists, there are plenty of specialized subjects to choose from, and lists to subscribe to.

? What Is a Listserver?
Every mailing list has a listserver – a remote computer that manages all the messages sent to it. A listserver has two main functions. It maintains a list of users and addresses, adding or deleting members to/from its database as they subscribe/unsubscribe. Secondly, it receives all e-mail messages contributed to the group, and then "reflects" them to all the other members. In this way, everybody receives a copy of all messages, but they need only send one to contact everyone else.

SUBSCRIBING TO A MAILING LIST
Subscribing to a mailing list simply involves e-mailing a listserver with a message telling it that you want to join. There will be a precise syntax that you need to use in your e-mail when subscribing, and you will need to find out this information before you can join (see "The Information You Need" below). Fortunately, there are many sites on the Web that provide this sort of information (see "Where to Look" on the right). Unsubscribing is done in the same way – by e-mailing the listserver with a specific message.

The Information You Need
For each list there are two e-mail addresses: the listserver and the list itself. Make sure that you send your subscription to the listserver. For example, to subscribe to the Sea Turtle Conservation *list, you would send an e-mail message to* **listserv@ nervm.nerdc.ufl.edu** *and type* sub CTURTLE your name *as the text. (Replace* **your name** *with your real name.)*

Where to Look
To find out about all the mailing lists that operate on the Internet, and how to join them, look at this site on the Web:
http://www.tile.net.

Subject Search
This site allows you to run a search for a list on a specific topic.

What's There?
The Tile site categorizes mailing lists by name and by subject. It also has a brief description of each, making it easy to find out if there is a list that interests you.

CTURTLE

Sea Turtle Biology and Conservation

Country: **USA**
Site: **NE Regional Data Center, Univ. of Florida campus, Gainesville FL**
Computerized administrator: listserv@nervm.nerdc.ufl.edu
Human administrator: cturtle-request@nervm.nerdc.ufl.edu

You can join this group by sending the message "*sub CTURTLE your name*" to listserv@nervm.nerdc.ufl.edu

Finding Files with E-Mail

Electronic mail also offers a simple and effective way to search for files on the Internet. Page 43 introduced you to an application called Archie, whose database of files and FTP sites you can search on-line. You can also search Archie using electronic mail, although the process is neither simple nor quick, and it can take a couple of hours to get a reply from Archie by e-mail.

If you don't want to be tied to your computer screen, however, sending an e-mail to Archie allows you to continue with other things while the search is in progress. Eventually, Archie will return an e-mail message containing details of the files and FTP sites that matched your search criteria. When you have received your reply, you can use your Web browser or FTP program to download those files.

The steps on this page show how to carry out an Archie search by e-mail for all files called "eudora."

Note How to Unsubscribe!
Some mailing lists can generate hundreds of messages per day and can swamp you with e-mail. Make sure that you keep a copy of the command for unsubscribing to a list so that you can cancel your subscription easily. You will find this information in one of the first messages that you receive after joining. To avoid excessive e-mail, it is advisable not to subscribe to too many mailing lists at any one time.

1 Open your e-mail program, (in this example *Microsoft Exchange*), and type **archie@** followed by the address of a local Archie server in the *To* box. Leave the subject field of your e-mail blank. If your program requires messages to have a subject, just type a space.

2 In the first line of your message, type **set mailto** followed by your e-mail address.

3 In the rest of your e-mail, type the details of your search using commands that Archie will understand (see box below). Type each command on a new line. Finally, type **quit**.

4 Send the message, in this case by clicking the *Send* button. Your answer will arrive by e-mail when Archie has conducted the search.

Additional Archie Commands

If you sent Archie a query exactly as described above, you'd receive a very long list of possible matches. To cut down on endless streams of unwanted or irrelevant files and sites, you can make your search more efficient with Archie's set of parameters. You type these extra commands into the message of your e-mail. The table to the right outlines some of the more common commands that you can use. If you need more detailed information on Archie commands and protocol, try sending your first query with just the word "help" in the body of the message (see steps above). The reply should also contain a list of Archie servers.

Command	Definition
find	❏ Type **find** *filename* (replace *filename* with the file you are looking for) to search for all files containing this name.
set search exact	❏ If you want to limit your search to an exact filename (for example, *eudora.exe*), type **set search exact eudora.exe**.
set search sub	❏ If you want your search to include all files containing a certain string of characters (for example, all files containing the letters "eudo"), type **set search sub eudo**.
maxhits	❏ To prevent Archie from sending you very large lists of "hits," type **maxhits** *number* (replace *number* with a suitable figure). For example, to limit the number of hits to 50, type **maxhits 50**.

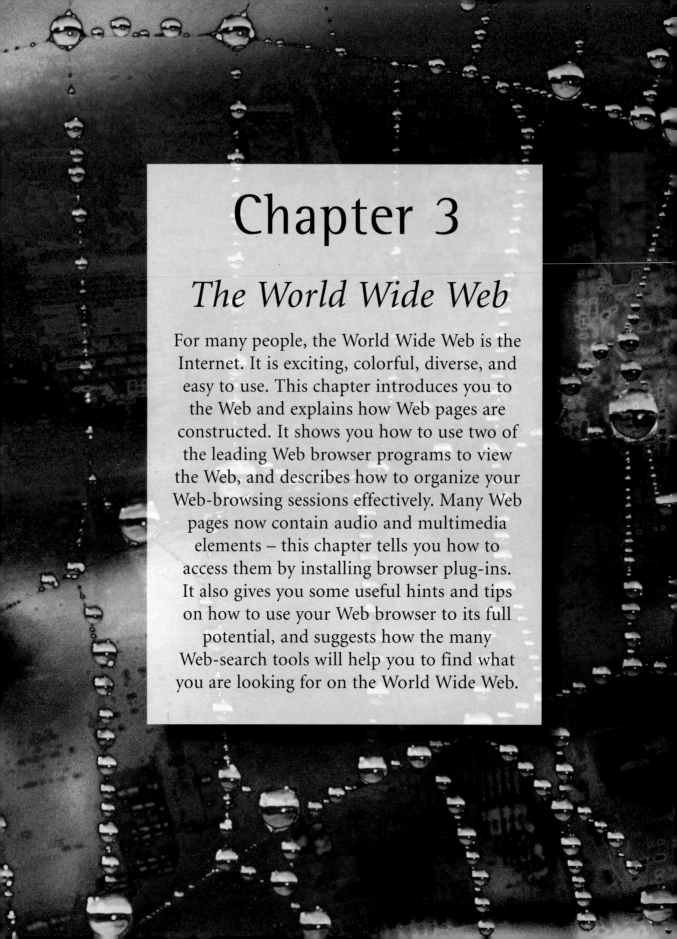

Chapter 3

The World Wide Web

For many people, the World Wide Web is the Internet. It is exciting, colorful, diverse, and easy to use. This chapter introduces you to the Web and explains how Web pages are constructed. It shows you how to use two of the leading Web browser programs to view the Web, and describes how to organize your Web-browsing sessions effectively. Many Web pages now contain audio and multimedia elements – this chapter tells you how to access them by installing browser plug-ins. It also gives you some useful hints and tips on how to use your Web browser to its full potential, and suggests how the many Web-search tools will help you to find what you are looking for on the World Wide Web.

3

What Is the Web?

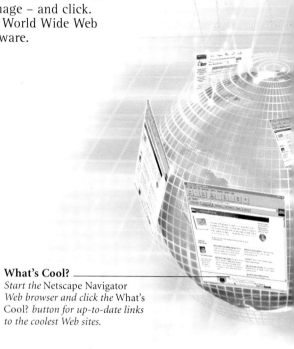

FOR THE MAJORITY OF INTERNET USERS, the World Wide Web (WWW or W3) is by far the most exciting aspect of the Internet. It is certainly the fastest-growing area, with an estimated 15–20 million "Web pages" to visit, and with thousands more appearing every month. The Web, as it is usually called, is a universe of linked "pages." A typical Web page contains words and pictures – often like a magazine page – but with one major difference: the information is interactive. Navigating the Web is much like using a multimedia CD-ROM. If you want to find out more information you point the mouse at a "live" area of the screen – usually a highlighted piece of text or an image – and click. This takes you to a new screen. All you need to access the World Wide Web is a standard Internet connection and some "browser" software.

Using the Web

The pages of the World Wide Web cover a vast range of topics. This alone has made it extremely popular. Perhaps the main advantage of using the Web is that it is easier to navigate, and can present information in a much more attractive way, than other Internet alternatives. A Web page can contain text, images, sounds, video clips and – most important of all – links to other pages. The Web can also be used to fetch documents or files from other types of Internet sites.

WEB BROWSER SOFTWARE
To access the Web you must first install some Web browser software. There are many alternative browsers to choose from, although the majority of Web users today are using *Netscape Navigator* or Microsoft's *Internet Explorer.* With the appropriate "plug-ins" and "helper" applications (see pages 68-73) you can also view animations and video clips, and hear sound files or even "live" audio broadcasts. Most of the popular Web browsers can be downloaded easily as shareware or freeware from FTP or Web sites.

What's Cool?
Start the Netscape Navigator *Web browser and click the* What's Cool? *button for up-to-date links to the coolest Web sites.*

Origins of the Web

The World Wide Web is the brainchild of CERN (European Laboratory for Particle Physics) engineer Tim Berners-Lee, who had the idea of creating an electronic web of research information. During the 1980s he developed a programming language called Hypertext Mark-up Language (HTML), on which the Web is based (see page 61). Early Web pages tended to be text-based, but since the rapid expansion of the Web in 1994, they have become capable of holding rich graphical and multimedia elements (see examples on the right).

A Text-Based Web Page

A Recent Web Page with Graphics

WHAT CAN I USE THE WEB FOR?

**http://www.netscape.com/
home/internet-search.html**

Research

For anyone interested in the research potential of the Internet, the Web is a highly attractive proposition. Many academic, government, and commercial organizations publish authoritative information on the Web. The Web also holds thousands of pages of information produced by enthusiasts – not always so reliable. Using one of the many Web-based search engines such as AltaVista, Infoseek, or Yahoo! (see pages 76-9), you can type a keyword to search for a list of Web sites that match your criteria.

**http://mmnewsstand.com/
index.html**

Commercial Activity

When the Internet began to reach main-stream users at the beginning of the 1990s, commercial activities were frowned upon by the existing Net community. This has changed dramatically, as businesses have realized that they have a huge customer base just waiting to be serviced. Consequently, Web sites advertising new products or offering home-shopping facilities have begun to take off. For example, a company's Web page may consist of a catalog of products for sale: clicking an item from the list will take you to a Web page dedicated to that product.

http://www.mtv.com

Entertainment

Whether your interests include computer games, karate, or juggling, somewhere you will find a Web site run by another enthusiast. Fans of all sorts are among the most entertaining presence on the Web. Some of the biggest names in the world of music, for example, have hundreds of Web sites dedicated to them by fans. Most media companies, record labels, and games companies offer information and free samples at their Web sites.

**http://www.teleport.com/
~mushin**

Personal Interests

One of the most attractive aspects of being on the Net is quite simply to enjoy the sense of being a part of its global community. Many Web users set up home pages for fun, usually providing personal histories of themselves and the things they like to do. This approach can be used for more practical purposes – for example, an increasing number of professional users create Web pages that act as an on-line personal resumé.

Best of the Web
On the start page for Microsoft's Internet Explorer at **http://home.microsoft.com***, click the Best of the Web tab to access a regularly updated directory of the best sites on the Web.*

SURFING THE WEB

The first time you visit the Web, you will probably want to look around and get a feel for what is available. Two pages on Netscape's site provide excellent starting points: the "What's New" and "What's Cool" pages. These give you lists of new and interesting sites, with a brief description of each page and the relevant URLs. These jump-off pages are at **home.netscape.com/home/whats-new.html** and **home.netscape.com/home/whats-cool.html** respectively. Most Web pages contain links to many other pages, so you will soon find yourself jumping from one site to another.

What Happens on a Web Page?

Web pages come in many different varieties. At their simplest, they contain static information – simple text. At the other end of the scale, the more adventurous sites are highly colorful, containing animation, sound, and interactive elements. As well as being entertaining and informative, many Web pages allow you to download your favorite pictures, sounds, and videoclips. Most contain links that connect you to a related page on the same site or on other Web sites. From some you can download files or software – a lot of excellent shareware can be obtained this way. Most will also contain e-mail addresses, enabling you to contact the producer or producers of the page directly.

WHAT IS A TYPICAL WEB PAGE?

There is really no such thing as a typical Web page, but the page shown on the right (which is from the Epicurious site at **http://www.epicurious.com**) is a good example of a colorful, well-organized site. This example contains textual and graphical links to other pages, an interactive on-line reference work, a database of recipes, and a facility for e-mailing favorite recipes to friends.

Eating | Drinking | Playing | Bon Appétit | Gourmet | Home | Text-Only Home

epicurious
E A T I N G

The Essential Restaurant Guide
A city-by-city survey of the best bites in town

A Linked Lexicon
Feed here, and you'll never have to eat your words

Recipe File
Tell us what you're craving – and whether it's lemon tea cake or lamb tagine, we'll tell you how to make it

ALSO FEATURED

Food for Love: A rich sampler of Valentine's Day menus, recipes for two, cocktail and champagne suggestions - and; a loving postcard from Jane and Michael Stern

Images and Buttons
Images, buttons, and icons often provide links to other Web pages or sites. Some images (especially maps) will contain a number of links. You can usually tell if an image provides a link because your mouse pointer changes its shape when moved over the relevant area.

In-Text Links
Click here to move to another Web page or site. "Hot" text usually appears in a different color from the main text and is often underlined.

Identifying a Web Site

Every Web site has a unique address. This address is referred to as a URL – Uniform (or Universal) Resource Locator. URLs for Web sites are always prefixed with the letters **http://**. Http is an abbreviation for HyperText Transport Protocol. Here is a breakdown of a typical URL:

www
The name of an organization's designated Web server. It is standard practice to name the Web server "www," although there are many possible variations.

/home.html
*Anything following the slash mark after the zone denotes the directory path on the server. This is the hierarchy of folders that eventually reaches the file that you want to open. In this example the file name is **home**. The final extension denotes that the file is an HTML file.*

Web Addresses
Most of the time, you navigate the Web by clicking on buttons, images, or text that provide a link to another Web page. However, take care when you enter an address (URL) manually. A URL can never contain spaces, and is case and punctuation sensitive. Although Web addresses usually comprise lower-case letters, some may contain capitals. In the example on the left, "superserve" would not be recognized if you typed **Superserve**.

http://www.superserve.com/home.html

http://
This indicates to your browser that you are going to connect to a Web document rather than, for example, an FTP or Gopher site. The letters "http" are always followed by a colon and two forward slashes.

.superserve
The name of the host or domain. This is the organization on whose computers the Web page resides.

.com
This indicates that superserve is a commercial organization. The final suffix – known as the zone name – indicates the type of organization (see page 49).

How Do Web Pages Work?

Each Web page is a "hypertext" document. Hypertext is not a piece of software; it is a term coined by 1950s computer visionary Ted Nelson. In practice, it means that a piece of text within one document may have a pointer to other pieces of text, either within the same document or on an external document.

Nearly all Web pages are created using Hypertext Mark-up Language (HTML) – one of the simplest computer languages ever created. HTML is a set of instructions inserted into plain text by the programmer.

USING HTML

To create an HTML document, text is sandwiched between a series of commands, or "tags." These tags control the way in which the text is presented when viewed with a Web browser. They are set up between pairs of brackets and do not appear when you view a Web page.

<TITLE>
The name of the HTML document. This becomes a part of the page's address.

<BODY>
The lines of text between <BODY> at the top and </BODY> at the bottom of the document contain all the HTML formatting tags.

<HTML>
This line tells the browser that the file is a hypertext mark-up document.

<HR>
This draws a thick horizontal line the width of the page, irrespective of the screen size at which the browser has been set.

<H1>
A font size is specified by the using the header commands. The largest size is <H1>, the smallest is <H6>.

<IMG SRC>
This places an image (named LENNON.GIF in this example) on the page. The ALIGN=TOP command lines up the top of the image with the line of the text.

<I>
The selected text is italicized. Like all pairing HTML commands, the instruction is switched off by inserting a slash in the second command: </I>.

Viewing the Code
Most of the leading Web browsers allow you to view the HTML code "behind" the Web page. In *Netscape Navigator*, for example, choose *Document Source* from the *View* menu to see the HTML coding for the page currently in your browser window.

Using a Web Browser

A FEW YEARS AGO, A WEB BROWSER WAS SIMPLY A TOOL for viewing the pages of the Web. Today's leading Web browsers have become much more than Web navigation tools: they have developed into all-in-one Internet "launchpads" from which you can send e-mail, visit newsgroups, run Telnet sessions, and access FTP and Gopher sites. Much of the sophistication of today's leading Web browsers is below the surface, since the browsers can automatically run many of the latest Web applications by using "helper" applications or "plug-ins" (see pages 68-73). This section describes the two leading Web browsers, Netscape Corporation's *Netscape Navigator* and Microsoft's *Internet Explorer*, showing you how to navigate the Web, use bookmarks to mark interesting sites, and install some of the most exciting multimedia plug-ins.

Getting the Latest Browser
The Web browser market is extremely competitive, with the two main producers – Microsoft and Netscape – releasing new "beta" versions every few weeks. You can download these test versions and find the latest information on *Netscape Navigator* from Netscape's Web site at **http://www.netscape.com**, and on *Internet Explorer* from Microsoft's site at **http://www.microsoft.com**. This book features version 3 of each browser.

Microsoft Internet Explorer

Microsoft's *Internet Explorer* first appeared in 1995 and has since been regularly enhanced. It is likely to become a serious contender with *Netscape Navigator* (see pages 64–5) in the Web browser market, especially since it is integrated with later versions of the Windows operating system. The illustration on this page shows the *Internet Explorer* browser window and describes some of the features that you will need to know for your first browsing session. Once you have come to grips with the browser's basic functions, you can access further features and fine-tune the settings of the browser from the menus and *Options* dialog boxes. It is worth exploring these, and reading the help files supplied with the program or available via Microsoft's Web site.

Address Box
This box displays the URL of the site currently open in Internet Explorer.

Main Browser Window
The main window of all Web browsers shows the pages that make up the Web. Hot links on these pages appear as colored, underlined text. Images, icons, and maps can also function in this way. The mouse pointer will change its shape when it is held over a hot link.

Home Page
Internet Explorer's *default home page is* **http://home.microsoft.com**. *Click the various tabs on this page to access directories of Web sites, information about Microsoft and Internet Explorer, or open the* MSN *home page. (You can customize this page to include hot links of your own.)*

Status Bar
This bar shows information relating to the current Web page, such as the names of image files that are being downloaded.

Opening picture: ie_msndn.gif at home.microsoft.com

Back
Displays the last Web page you viewed. Using Back *repeatedly will return you to other pages visited in the current session.*

Forward
The Forward *button will return you to the page or pages you were viewing when you first clicked* Back.

Stop
Halts the transfer of data over the Internet. This can be useful if you can see a link you want but images are still downloading.

Refresh
Loads a fresh copy of the current Web page. If you have used Stop, *for example,* Refresh *will reload the page in its entirety.*

Home
Takes you back to Explorer's home page. You can specify any Web site as your home page in View/Options.

Search
Searches for Web sites that match your criteria, using the main Internet search engines.

Favorites
See pages 66–7.

Print
Prints the page currently in your active browser window.

Font
Changes the size of the font of the page shown in the browser window.

Mail
See "Mail and News Features" on this page.

KNOW YOUR HISTORY

The *Go* menu lists all the sites visited in the current session. Alternatively, choose *Show History Folder* to open a folder that provides shortcuts to sites visited in previous sessions.

Links

Clicking the Links *button on the toolbar replaces the* Address *box with a new toolbar. This provides links to Microsoft and Web support pages, as well as information about new or topical Web sites. Click* Address *when you want to revert to the default tool bar.*

Changing Your Options

If your browser is running slowly, you can speed it up by choosing not to load certain types of files automatically. Do this by choosing *Options* from the *View* menu. On the *General* page, for example, you can choose not to display images when viewing a Web page by unchecking the *Show Pictures* box.

MAIL AND NEWS FEATURES

Internet Explorer 3 contains built-in mail and news programs, called *Internet Mail* and *Internet News,* that you can access from the browser. When you first run them, you are guided through a simple set-up routine that prompts you for details about your service provider's news and mail servers (see checklist on page 33).

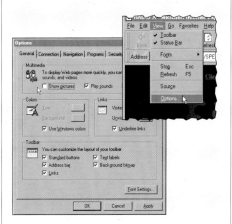

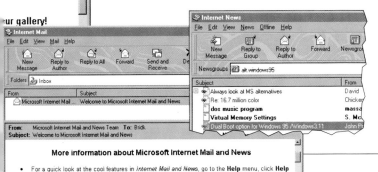

More information about Microsoft Internet Mail and News

* For a quick look at the cool features in *Internet Mail and News,* go to the **Help** menu, click **Help Topics,** and then look up **features** in the index.
* If you've set up your Mail or Newsreader accounts with your service provider but are having

Netscape Navigator

For some time, *Netscape Navigator* has been the most widely used Web browser in the world, with Microsoft's *Internet Explorer* steadily gaining popularity. In most respects these browsers work in similar ways. However, as far as users are concerned, the most important issue is deciding which of the many browsers available they feel happiest with. In fact, there is no reason why you should not run more than one browser on your computer: many users do.

While each Web browser has its own unique features, the basic navigation tools available from the main browser window are very similar. This page describes the main features and shortcuts available from *Netscape Navigator*'s main window. From the default home page (see right), you can download the latest version of the browser (but remember to read the licensing document first).

THE OPTIONS MENU

By selecting items from the *Options* menu you can alter the way in which information is displayed on the screen. In *General Preferences*, you can specify the size of font and color of text on the Web page you are viewing, as well as other options. Many advanced browser features may be customized via the *Options* menu.

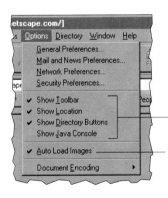

Display Options
The menu bar at the top of the window is the only part of Navigator's screen that has to be displayed. You can choose not to display the main toolbar, location box, and directory buttons.

Image Display
Some heavily illustrated Web pages can take a long time to download. Switching off Auto Load Images will stop pictures from being displayed automatically.

Other Web Browsers

Between them, *Internet Explorer* and *Netscape Navigator* have captured approximately 95 percent of the Web-browser market. However, there are several other programs that are capable of performing the basic functions just as well. Probably the most popular of these browsers is NCSA's *Mosaic*. This was the original Web browser, and new versions of the program continue to be made available. You can download *Mosaic* from **ftp://ftp.ncsa.uiuc.edu**.

THE NAVIGATOR WINDOW

In *Netscape Navigator*, the toolbar and buttons at the top of the browser window perform similar functions to those in other browsers. For example, there are *Forward* and *Back* buttons for viewing pages you have accessed during a session, a *Reload* button for refreshing the page you are currently viewing, and so on. This illustration shows some other essential features of this browser.

Home
Click the Home button to return to your home page. You can change your home site by choosing General Preferences in the Options menu. Click the Appearance tab and type the URL of a new site. Some users prefer to have a blank home screen. This allows Navigator to run without an Internet connection in place.

Quick Links
This button is used for saving "bookmarks" (see pages 66–7).

Location Bar
This contains the URL of the Web site currently displayed. By typing a new address and pressing the Return key, you jump to a different site.

Directory Buttons
This optional set of buttons contains links to a number of useful Netscape directories:
- What's New? – *details of new Web sites*
- What's Cool? – *Netscape's own selection of interesting or innovative Web pages*
- Destinations – *Netscape's directory of Web sites, organized by categories*
- Net Search – *links to major search engines and Web directories*
- People – *a selection of e-mail search directories*
- Software – *directories of downloadable software, upgrades, and plug-ins*

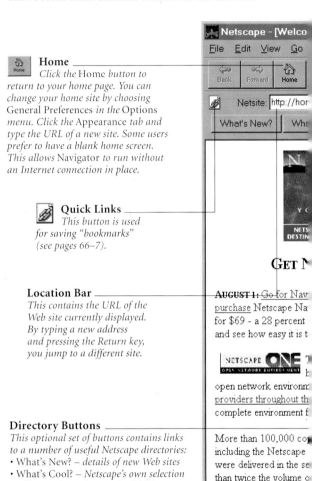

Status Bar
This provides useful details about your connection, such as the rate of data transmission.

Open
Click here to access the Open box. Type a URL in this box and press Return to connect to that site.

Find
Click this button to search for a specified piece of text on the current Web page.

Previous Pages
Click this arrow to access a drop-down menu containing the URLs of Web pages viewed during the current session. You can click on any of these URLs to recall the page.

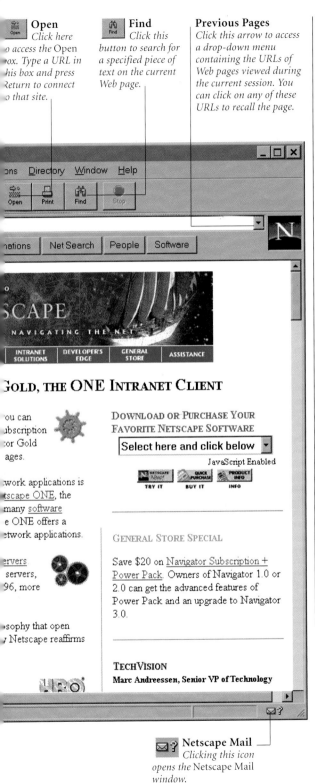

Netscape Mail
Clicking this icon opens the Netscape Mail *window.*

Netscape News and Mail

Netscape Navigator comes with its own newsreader and mail programs. Before you can use these from your Web browser, you need to configure them, but this is a simple procedure (see "Configuring Mail and News" below). You access the *Mail* and *News* windows from the *Window* menu.

Netscape Mail

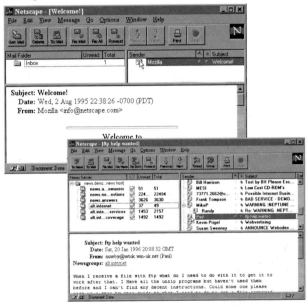

Netscape News

CONFIGURING MAIL AND NEWS

Before you first use these programs, access the browser's *Options* menu and choose *Mail and News Preferences*. On the *Identity* page, type your name and e-mail address in the boxes provided. Then click the *Servers* tab and type the name of your service provider's mail and news servers (see page 33) in the appropriate boxes. The *Mail* and *News* programs are now ready to use.

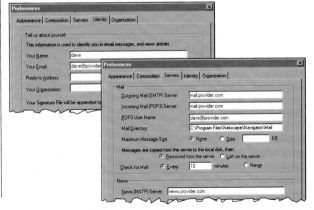

Bookmarking Your Favorite Pages

A lengthy browsing session on the Web can take you to dozens or even hundreds of sites, so you'll need a way of noting the sites you wish to return to later. Trying to find a page you saw "earlier" during a session can be time-consuming and frustrating if you have forgotten to make a note of it. Fortunately, most browsers include a "bookmark" feature that you can access quickly from the menu bar or toolbar. The bookmark feature usually allows you to organize bookmarks into hierarchical drop-down menus for easy access while you are on-line. This page will show you how to create and manage your bookmarks in both *Netscape Navigator* and Microsoft's *Internet Explorer*.

MANAGING FAVORITES IN INTERNET EXPLORER

Managing favorites in *Internet Explorer* is like managing folders in *Windows 95*. Once you have opened the *Favorites* folder (choose *Open Favorites Folder* from the *Favorites* menu) you can create a logical structure for storing your favorite places by making new folders, dragging and dropping items, and deleting old or obsolete items. Because *Internet Explorer* prompts you to file favorites as you create them, minimal management is usually required.

When you first install *Internet Explorer*, it imports any bookmarks relating to other Web browsers on your PC into its own *Favorites* folder. You access these bookmarks by choosing *Imported Bookmarks* from the *Favorites* menu.

CREATING FAVORITES IN INTERNET EXPLORER

In *Internet Explorer*, bookmarks are called "favorites." The steps below show how to create and then view a favorite.

1 When you are browsing a page you would like to bookmark, choose *Add to Favorites* from the *Favorites* menu.

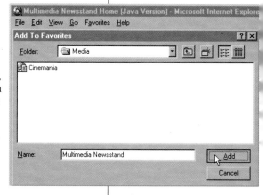

2 In the *Add To Favorites* dialog box, navigate to the folder in which you want to store the favorite, type a name for it in the *Name* box ("Multimedia Newsstand" in this example), and then click *Add*. You can create a new folder by clicking the *New Folder* button on the toolbar.

3 You can now access this favorite by using the *Favorites* menu. The favorite created in these steps appears in a drop-down menu that corresponds to the folder where it was saved. Choose its name from the menu to open that site in the browser.

Favorite Properties
You can find out more information about a favorite by right-clicking on its name in the folder where it is stored, and choosing Properties *from the drop-down menu.*

MANAGING BOOKMARKS IN NAVIGATOR
In *Netscape Navigator* you can organize and edit your bookmark entries by choosing *Bookmarks* from the *Window* menu. By accessing the menus in the *Bookmarks* window, you can add, delete, organize, and edit all your current bookmarks. For example, from the *Item* menu, you can add and name new folders and then drag and drop existing bookmarks into them. The contents of these new folders will appear as submenu items when you next access the *Bookmarks* menu in the browser window.

If you keep the *Bookmarks* window open throughout a Web session, you can manage your bookmarks as you go along. When you create bookmarks by using the *Add Bookmark* command, they are added to the bottom of the list. With the *Bookmarks* window already open, you can drag and drop new entries directly into a suitable folder by using the *Quick Link* feature (see the steps on this page).

CREATING BOOKMARKS IN NETSCAPE NAVIGATOR
These are some of the ways you can create bookmarks in *Netscape Navigator:*

❑ Use the *Add Bookmark* command from the *Bookmarks* menu

❑ Cut and paste a URL from the *Go to* box into the *Bookmarks* window

❑ Use the *Quick Link* button

The steps below show how to create and then view a bookmark using the *Quick Link* button.

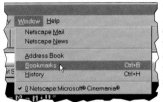

1 While browsing the page you want to bookmark, choose *Bookmarks* from the *Window* menu. This will open the *Bookmarks* window where all your bookmarks are displayed.

2 Position the *Bookmarks* window so that it doesn't obscure the *Quick Link* icon. Click this icon and hold down the mouse button.

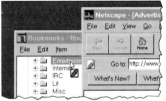

3 Keep holding down the mouse button and drag from the *Quick Link* icon across to the *Bookmark* window. A new icon will appear under your mouse pointer. Release the mouse when it is directly over the destination folder.

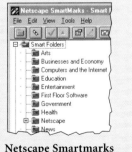

4 You can now access this bookmark directly from the *Bookmarks* menu. Navigate through the submenus until you reach the one that corresponds to the folder where you stored the bookmark. Then choose the bookmark to open that site in the browser.

EXTRA HELP WITH BOOKMARKS
The more you use a Web browser, the longer and more unwieldy your list of bookmarks is likely to become. There are programs available to help you manage them more efficiently. *Netscape Smartmarks,* for example, structures bookmarks in hierarchical folders. It also supplies you with a large number of useful addresses, and monitors specified Web sites to inform you if anything has changed since your last visit.

Netscape Smartmarks
For more information on *Smartmarks*, visit the Netscape site at **http://www.netscape.com.**

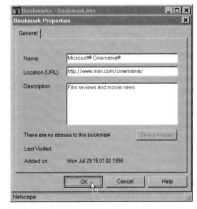

Bookmark Properties
To find more information about a bookmarked page (for example, its URL and the date you last visited it), click the bookmark's name in the Bookmarks *window, and then choose* Properties *from the* Item *menu.*

Multimedia on the Web

WEB PAGES WERE ONCE VERY SIMILAR TO MAGAZINE PAGES: they consisted of laid-out text and images, and were essentially static. Today, many Web pages are multimedia creations, full of sound, movement, and interactivity. With the latest Web browsers you can experience animations, tickertape text, live audio and video, and interactive games. Since 1995, the Web has been brought to life by new technologies, especially *JAVA* and *ActiveX* (see box opposite), and applications such as *Shockwave* and *RealAudio*. This section provides a showcase for some of the most exciting multimedia features you will find on the Web and explains how you can access them using your Web browser.

Web Browsers and Multimedia

All Web browsers can display HTML-formatted text and most image files, but the latest versions of *Netscape Navigator* and Microsoft's *Internet Explorer* can also automatically handle a number of audio, video, and 3-D file formats (see "Preinstalled Browser Plug-Ins" opposite). Since there are so many different file formats on the Internet, most Web browsers are designed to handle only the most common ones automatically. Fortunately, both the Web browsers shown here can be enhanced to handle more unusual file types by installing "plug-ins."

A plug-in is simply a program that adds capabilities to your browser – for example, the ability to handle video, animation, games, and interactive documents. If your Web browser encounters an unknown data type on a Web page, it looks for an installed plug-in that can handle that type. If it finds one, it launches it automatically. If not, you will need to download the appropriate plug-in (see pages 70-1).

ANIMATION
This animated sequence – on DK's Web site at **http://www.dk.com** – was produced using the animated GIF (GIF 89a) format. A GIF 89a file can contain a number of separate images that are cycled to give the appearance of animation. The latest Web browsers need no additional plug-ins to show this file type.

SOUND
Many pages contain "streamed" sound files. For example, the Independent Underground Music Archive site at **http://www.iuma.com** offers sound files in several formats, including *RealAudio*.

VIDEO
Video can now be played without having to download large files to your hard disk first. Some of the newer browsers handle streamed video, playing a little at a time as it is received over the Internet. This clip from the multimedia showcase at **http://www.wintermute.net/pic.html** is displayed using *CoolFusion* – a preinstalled Netscape plug-in.

Preinstalled Browser Plug-Ins

The latest versions of both *Netscape Navigator* and *Internet Explorer* come with certain plug-ins preinstalled. *Netscape Navigator* includes, for example, *Live3D* (a VRML program that displays interactive 3-D images), and *LiveAudio* (a sound player with volume and playback controls). *Internet Explorer* offers a movie player called *ActiveMovie*, which uses Microsoft's own *ActiveX* system (see box below). You can further enhance your browser's capabilities by downloading and installing new browser plug-ins (see pages 70-1).

3-D GRAPHICS

A VRML program (Virtual Reality Modeling Language) enables you to explore virtual worlds and manipulate three-dimensional images on the Internet. This example shows *Viscape*, by Superscape. You can download this plug-in from **http://www.superscape.com**.

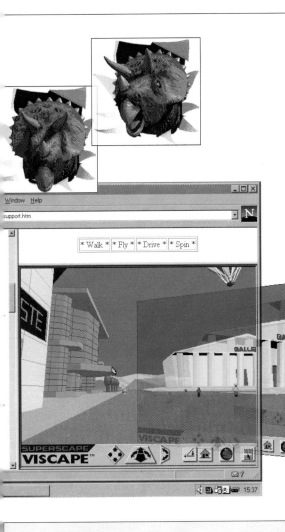

What Is JAVA?

JAVA is a programming language that enables Web pages to contain miniature programs – called applets – that appear as animation, sound, scrolling text, or interactive features such as functional spreadsheets. This enhancement has revolutionized the way the Web is perceived both by developers and users. Your Web browser needs to be *JAVA*-enhanced if you want to view *JAVA* applets. Both browsers featured in this book have built-in *JAVA* capabilities.

What Is ActiveX?

ActiveX controls are similar to *JAVA* applets in that they add the same kinds of capability to your Web browser. The difference is that when you encounter an *ActiveX control* on a Web page you will be asked whether you wish to download it to your hard disk. If you accept, the *ActiveX control* will automatically download and configure itself. It is then integrated into your operating system, becoming active each time it is required on a Web page, and launching the appropriate program or file.

NAVIGATING IN 3-D

In the example shown above, you have a 360-degree range of movement. Use the controls (shown below) at the bottom of the window to travel around the screen.

Move
Move vertically up or down, and horizontally left or right.

Direction
Go left, right, back, or forward.

Look Up/Down
Move your view up or down.

Installing New Plug-Ins

To use a new browser plug-in, you need to download the plug-in software – usually from the software developer's home page – and install it on your hard disk. The developer's home page may point you to other Web sites where you can see the plug-in being used.

Most plug-ins are self-extracting files that are very easy to install. During installation, you will be prompted to confirm the folder you wish to store the software in, and may be asked for some registration details. You may also be asked which Web browser, or browsers, you intend to use the plug-in with. (Some installation programs locate the Web browser, or browsers, on your hard disk and ask you to confirm installation for each one.)

DOWNLOADING SHOCKWAVE

Macromedia's *Shockwave* is a typical example of an easy-to-install browser plug-in. If you visit sites containing *Shockwave* files, you will be able to view animation and "streamed" movies, use clickable buttons, and hear high-quality sound. Streamed sound and video starts to play while the file is being downloaded, rather than waiting for the whole file to be downloaded. The steps on these pages show how to download and install the *Shockwave* plug-in. First go to Macromedia's home page at **http://www.macromedia.com** and follow the steps below.

Shortcuts to Plug-Ins

If you are using *Netscape Navigator* and you reach a Web page requiring a plug-in that is not installed on your computer, you will often see a jigsaw puzzle piece icon. When you click this icon, the *Plugin Not Loaded* dialog box pops up. Clicking the *Get the Plugin* button in this dialog box takes you to a Netscape page that tells you where to find the plug-in.

Jigsaw Icon
This icon tells you that you need a specific plug-in.

Get the Plugin
Clicking this button takes you to a site from which you can download a required plug-in.

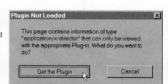

If you use *Internet Explorer* and access a page containing *ActiveX* content, you may see an Authenticode "security certificate" that identifies the source of the program and the name of its developer. If you are unsure about the integrity of the source or the data, you can choose not to download the control.

1 On Macromedia's home page, click *Download Shockwave.*

2 On the page that appears, type your name and e-mail address (this is optional). Click the arrow next to *Which platform do you use?* and choose *Windows95/NT* from the drop-down menu. Click the *Get Shockwave* button.

3 On the next page, click one of the listed FTP sites. The *Save As* dialog box will appear. Choose a folder in which to save the *Shockwave* installation program and click *Save. Shockwave* will now be downloaded onto your hard disk.

INSTALLING SHOCKWAVE

The downloaded version of the *Shockwave* installation program is called N32z0005 in this example. (Later versions will have different names.) To begin installation, double-click this file. An MS-DOS window will appear while a file called **Setupex** is extracted from the original file. When "Finished" appears in the window's title bar, close the window, then follow these steps.

1 Double-click the *Setupex* icon. Click *Yes* in the dialog box that appears.

2 In the *Select Browser* dialog box, click the box next to the name of the browser you intend to use the plug-in with. Click *Next*.

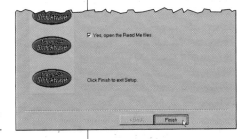

3 In the dialog box that appears, read the information in the *Destination Directory* panel. The correct directory should have been automatically detected. If it has not, click *Browse* and navigate to the correct directory. Finally, click *Next*.

4 In the *Setup Complete* dialog box, click *Finish* to complete the installation.

Do I Need All These Plug-Ins?

There are hundreds of plug-ins available for adding functionality to your Web browser, with new ones appearing regularly. Many plug-ins provide the same basic function (for example, playing video files). Some are only used by a small number of Web pages. Before downloading a plug-in, it is worth considering whether you really need the functionality that it offers.

Shockwave in Action

The Web site of New York-based multimedia company, MB Interactive, illustrates both the effectiveness of *Shockwave's* interactive capabilities and the high quality of the sound produced. The example here (found at **http://mbinter.com/ss7x7/jungle.htm**) features an interactive on-line rhythm machine with play and record capability. Clicking any button on the bottom row plays back a variety of continuous drum loops. The upper row introduces a series of ambient sounds that can be heard over the drum rhythm tracks. You can use the *Write* button to save a sequence of rhythms and sounds to your hard disk.

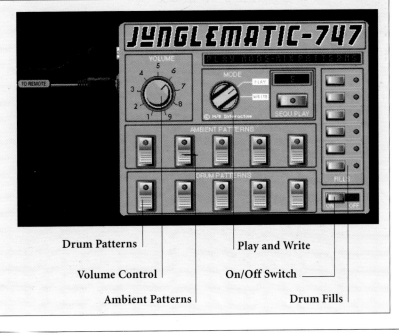

Drum Patterns | Play and Write

Volume Control | On/Off Switch

Ambient Patterns | Drum Fills

How Browsers Handle File Types

When your Web browser encounters any type of file on the Internet, it consults a small database of file formats to see whether it is capable of playing or displaying it. When you install a plug-in or *ActiveX control* this database is updated automatically. It is also possible to alter these settings or replace an existing helper application with one you prefer. For example, you might wish to play MPEG movie files using your favorite MPEG player rather than a player that has already been assigned. The examples below show how to review the file type settings in *Netscape Navigator* and Microsoft's *Internet Explorer.*

NETSCAPE NAVIGATOR
To access the *Helpers* page shown below, choose *General Preferences* from the *Options* menu, then click the *Helpers* tab in the *Preferences* dialog box.

File Type
This column shows the file type, followed by the application name (known as MIME-type).

Action
This column shows the program associated with the file type. In this example RealAudio files are associated with the RealAudio player. If Ask User appears in this column, you will be prompted each time you encounter the associated file type on the Web. You can choose to launch the program associated with that file, or save the file to your hard disk. If the line is blank, no program is currently associated with it.

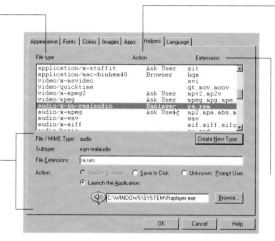

File Type Details
This information relates to the file type highlighted in the main box above. The program in this example – the RealAudio *player – will be launched automatically each time you click on a* RealAudio *file.*

File Extensions
This column shows file extensions associated with a particular file type. Some file types are associated with more than one extension.

INTERNET EXPLORER
To see the file types recognized by Microsoft's *Internet Explorer,* choose *Options* from the browser's *View* menu, then click *File Types* to display the *File Types* dialog box. Because *Internet Explorer* is designed to integrate as fully as possible with the *Windows 95* operating system, this dialog box relates to all *Windows 95* programs and not just *Internet Explorer.* This is evident from the fact that you can access the *File Types* dialog box from any open window on your desktop (by choosing *Options* from the *View* menu, then clicking the *File Types* tab in the *Options* dialog box).

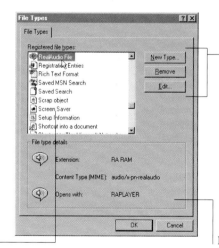

File Type Editing Buttons
You can use these buttons to add a new file type, or modify or delete currently registered file types. You should not attempt to do this unless you are an experienced Windows 95 *user. From this dialog box, any changes you make will relate to the whole* Windows 95 *environment and not just to* Internet Explorer.

Registered File Types
This window shows information about files that are currently registered. When a file is registered, Windows 95 *stores information relating to it, such as the file's extension, and the program assigned to open it.*

File Type Details
When you highlight any of the files in the Registered file types *window, the* File type details *panel will display information about the file's extension, its type, and the program (if any) that is used to open it.*

Plug-In Library

New plug-ins, and upgrades for existing ones, are appearing all the time on the Web. The best way to keep in touch with new developments is to visit one of the regularly updated plug-in lists on the Web. Netscape provides a list at **http://home.netscape.com/comprod/products/navigator/version_2.0/ plugins/index.html**.

This page shows a selection of the hundreds of *Windows 95*-compatible plug-ins that are available. After each plug-in you will see the address of a Web site from which you can download it or where you can find further information about the plug-in.

AUDIO AND VIDEO

• Crescendo
Produced by LiveUpdate, Crescendo allows you to play stereo MIDI music from the Web. This free plug-in has a CD-like control panel and digital counter.
http://www.liveupdate.com/midi.html

• Intervu MPEG Player
Intervu's MPEG Player *enables you to play MPEG audio-video files that are streamed as you download them. You can preview the first frame of the movie before downloading it.*
http://www.intervu.com/pavillion /product.html

• RapidTransit
Eastman's RapidTransit *decompresses and plays high-quality stereo streamed sound from Web pages.*
http//:www.monsterbit.com/rapidtransit/ RTPlayer.html

• MovieStar
The MovieStar *plug-in enables you to view Apple's* QuickTime *movies from a Web site.*
http//:www.monsterbit.com/rapidtransit/ RTPlayer.html

3-D AND ANIMATION

• CosmoPlayer
Produced by Silicon Graphics, CosmoPlayer *is a VRML viewer.*
http://vrml.sgi.com/cosmoplayer

• FutureSplash
Produced by Futurewave, you can use FutureSplash *to view animated graphics and drawings from the Web in real time.*
http://www.futurewave.com

• VRScout
This VRML plug-in from Chaco Communications enables you to interact with 3-D graphical locations and objects.
http://www.chaco.com/vrscout/ plugin.html

• Wirl Virtual Reality Browser
This advanced VRML plug-in from Vream is used on a number of Web pages that present interactive virtual worlds.
http://www.vream.com/3dl1.html

OTHER PLUG-INS

• AboutPeople
Now Software's AboutPeople *plug-in lets you browse and search address books.*
http://www.nowsoft.com/plugins/ plugins_download.html

• Acrobat Reader
Acrobat Reader *from Adobe allows you to view, navigate, and print* pdf *(Portable Document Format) file types.*
http://www.adobe.com/acrobat/3beta/ main.html

• Astound Web Player
Produced by Gold Disk Inc., Astound Web Player *allows you to view multimedia documents written using* Astound *or* Studio M *software from your browser.*
http://www.golddisk.com/awp/index.html

• Earthtime
Starfish Software's Earthtime *plug-in lets you view the time around the world. Its additional animated worldwide map also indicates daylight and darkness.*
http://www.starfishsoftware.com/ getearth.html

• FIGleaf
Produced by Carberry Technology, FIGleaf *enables your browser to view a wide variety of graphic formats (including* gif, jpg, png, cgm, tiff, ccitt, bmp, rgb, *and Sun Raster).*
http://www.ct.ebt.com/figinline/ download.htm

• Formula One/Net
Formula One/Net *from Visual Components allows you to view and operate* Microsoft Excel-*compatible spreadsheets over the Web.*
http://www.visualcomp.com/f1net/ download.htm

• Pointcast Network
PointCast Network *accesses a free service displaying constantly updated news, weather, financial news, sports, and other information.*
http://www.pointcast.com

• Shockwave for Freehand
This version of Macromedia's Shockwave *displays* Freehand *illustrations on the Web.*
http://www.macromedia.com/Tools/ Shockwave/Plugin/plugin.cgi

• Quick View Plus
This plug-in allows you to view, copy, print, and manage around 200 different file formats from within your browser.
http://www.inso.com/consumer/qvp /demo.htm

• Word Viewer
Inso Corporation's Word Viewer *displays* Microsoft Word 6.0 *or* 7.0 *documents in a Web browser. It allows you to copy and print them with the original formatting intact.*
http://www.inso.com/consumer/wordview/ plug.htm

Web Browser Hints and Tips

While *Netscape Navigator* and Microsoft's *Internet Explorer* are both extremely simple to use, you will soon find many ways to make the most of your computer's resources. By customizing the browser, and learning its mouse and keyboard shortcuts, you can access the Web more quickly and make your browsing sessions more secure.

Creating a Desktop Shortcut
You can create a desktop shortcut for any Internet site from your Web browser. To do this, simply click on a hot link and drag it from the browser window to the desktop. When you click this icon later, it will launch your default browser and attempt to open that page.

INCREASE YOUR DISK CACHE

When you visit a Web page, your browser saves text and images from the page to your hard disk in a folder called a "cache." When you next visit the site, this information in the cache is loaded directly from your disk, so that you don't need to download information each time. Increasing the size of your cache folder (to between 5 and 10 MB) can considerably speed up access to Web pages that you revisit, but too large a cache folder can be detrimental to your browser's performance.

Navigator
To increase the cache size, choose Network Preferences *from the* Options *menu and click the* Cache *tab. Type a new cache size (in kilobytes) in the* Disk Cache *box, and click* OK. *If you visit a large number of sites on a regular basis, you might want to try a disk cache of 10 MB.*

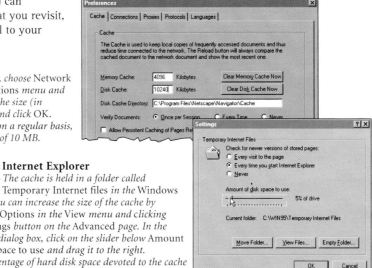

Internet Explorer
The cache is held in a folder called Temporary Internet files *in the* Windows *folder. You can increase the size of the cache by choosing* Options *in the* View *menu and clicking the* Settings *button on the* Advanced *page. In the* Settings *dialog box, click on the slider below* Amount of disk space to use *and drag it to the right. The percentage of hard disk space devoted to the cache is shown to the right of this slider. Finally, click* OK.

Keyboard Shortcuts

Although the graphical "point and click" interface makes navigating the World Wide Web very easy, you can save yourself a surprising amount of time by using keyboard shortcuts. Some shortcuts apply to specific browsers; others are common to several browsers (see examples on the right). You can use some *Windows 95* shortcuts for highlighted text – for example, Ctrl C copies highlighted text to the clipboard.

Internet Explorer and Netscape Navigator

 Ctrl N - Open a new browser window.

 Ctrl O - Open a file that you have saved to your hard disk.

 Ctrl S - Save this page to your hard disk.

 Ctrl F - Find (in this page).

 Escape - Stop this page from loading.

Internet Explorer

 F5 - Reload this page.

Netscape Navigator

 Ctrl R - Reload this page.

 Ctrl I - Load images on this page.

 Ctrl D - Add a bookmark for this page.

 Ctrl B - Open the bookmarks window.

Security Issues

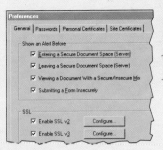

Some Web sites are termed "insecure," which means that your personal information – in most cases only your e-mail address – may be recorded. As a safety precaution, both browsers can be set up to prompt you with a security alert message. These messages warn you that you may be sending personal information over an insecure link – this is especially relevant to credit card transactions. You can view and adjust the security settings for your browser by accessing the dialog boxes shown on the right. Disabling your browser's security features is not recommended.

Navigator
To view the security settings for Netscape Navigator, *Choose* Security Preferences *from the* Options *menu.*

Internet Explorer
Choose Options *in the* View *menu and click the* Security *tab, to view the security options for this browser.*

USING POP-UP MENUS

Clicking the right mouse button over a hot link on a Web page generates a pop-up menu that provides you with a range of options. The content of each pop-up menu differs depending on the type of hot link you are accessing. The examples on the right show how to save an image to your hard disk.

Navigator
You can save an image quickly by positioning the cursor over the image, clicking the right-hand button, and choosing Save Image As. *In the* Save As *dialog box, type a name for the image and navigate to a suitable folder to save it in.*

Internet Explorer
You can save an image as desktop "wallpaper" by choosing Save As Wallpaper *from the drop-down menu.*

HANDLING COOKIES

A "cookie" (or "magic cookie," as it is sometimes known) is a short string of text that is generated when you visit certain types of Web sites; this text is downloaded onto your hard disk. The cookie holds temporary information that relates to that Web page, so that the information is in place when you next visit it. For example, if you visit a shopping Web site, the goods in your "shopping list" can be held until you next visit that site. If you are interested in knowing when cookies are being downloaded, you can have your browser alert you to the fact.

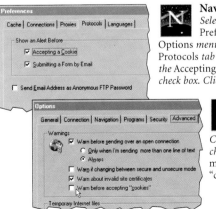

Navigator
Select Network Preferences *in the* Options *menu. Click the* Protocols *tab and click on the* Accepting a Cookie *check box. Click on OK.*

Internet Explorer
Choose Options *in the* View *menu. Click the* Advanced *tab and check the box marked* Warn me before accepting "cookies." *Then click OK.*

Searching the Web

WITH AT LEAST 20 MILLION INDIVIDUAL PAGES on the World Wide Web, the task of finding precisely what you are looking for may seem daunting. When you use one of the many search tools available on the Web, however, this task becomes more manageable. Many Web-based search tools can trawl Web sites, Gopher sites, and newsgroups, based on your search criteria. The more powerful search engines (some of which are described on these pages) can return the results of an Internet-wide search in a matter of seconds.

Search Tools

The two main types of search tools are Web directories and search engines. Web directories are well-organized lists of topics and subtopics through which you navigate to find a Web site that matches what you are looking for: this is much like consulting a huge index. Search engines are more powerful in that they do the searching for you by following the instructions you give them. The more detailed your instructions, the more accurate the results will be.

MAKING YOUR FIRST SEARCH
To use a search engine or directory, you open your Web browser and type its address. Performing a search varies little in principle from one search tool to another. You simply type a keyword, or series of keywords, which is used to generate a list of "hits": Web sites that contain those key words. This list usually contains a brief description of each site, along with its address. By clicking the address, you move directly to the chosen site.

Search Engines and Web Directories

One of the best starting points for searching the Internet is to use an all-in-one search page. Two of the best examples are provided by Netscape at **http://www.netscape.com/home/internet-search.html** and Microsoft at **http://www.msn.com/access/allinone.asp**.
From these pages you can link directly to many of the major search engines and directories. Here is a list of the principal search engines and Web directories, along with their URLs:

Search Engines

- AltaVista – **http://altavista.digital.com**
- Excite – **http://excite.com**
- Infoseek – **http://guide.infoseek.com**
- Lycos – **http://www.lycos.com**
- Opentext – **http://www.opentext.com**
- Webcrawler – **http://www.webcrawler.com**
- WWW Worm – **http://wwww.cs.colorado.edu/wwww**

Web Directories

- Accufind – **http://nin.com**
- Galaxy – **http://galaxy.einet.net**
- Magellan – **http://magellan.mckinley.com**
- Pointcom – **http://www.pointcom.com**
- YAHOO! – **http://www.yahoo.com**
- The Yellow Pages – **http://theyellowpages.com**

USING THE ALTAVISTA SEARCH ENGINE
This example shows how to use *Netscape Navigator* and Digital's *AltaVista* – one of the most popular search engines – to find Web sites relating to the Beatles.

1 Click the *Net Search* button. This takes you to *Netscape Navigator*'s all-in-one search page. Each time you click the *Net Search* button *Navigator* provides an entry screen to one of the search engines or directories, chosen at random. At the bottom of the page you will find hot links to all of the search tools.

2 Click on *AltaVista*. This connects you to the *AltaVista* home page.

3 Type **beatles** in the criteria box below *Search*, then click the *Submit* button.

4 *AltaVista* tells you how many related sites have been found, and lists the first ten in a scrolling window. To visit any of these sites, right-click on the title of the page, or its address, and choose *Open in New Window* from the drop-down menu that appears. The page will be displayed in a new browser window.

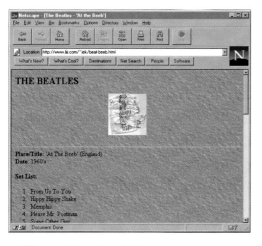

5 When you have viewed this page, close the Web browser window. You can now return to the *AltaVista* page displayed in the first browser window.

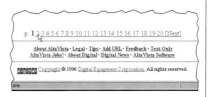

6 To look at the next page of ten URLs relating to your search, scroll to the bottom of the screen and click on *2*.

Can I Search Outside the Web?
Search engines are not only useful for trawling the World Wide Web – most of them can also search other areas of the Internet, such as Gopherspace and Usenet newsgroups. In *AltaVista*, for example, it is possible to restrict your search to only the Usenet newsgroups: before submitting your search, click the arrow alongside the *Search* box, and choose *Usenet* from the drop-down menu.

Choosing the Right Search Tool

With a large number of search engines and Web directories freely available, it is worth giving some thought to the tools which best suit your own needs. Different search tools can yield very different results for the same search criteria. This is because each search engine and Web directory uses different methods to update the information it holds on new Web sites.

Each search tool may also use different methods for carrying out your search. The *AltaVista* database, for example, holds details of almost every word on each Web page stored. Other directories may only hold details of the title or first line of text. The way in which the tools display the results differs as well. *Yahoo!*, for instance, provides a comment relating to each hit. By contrast, *AltaVista* hits display the first few lines of text on a page, which may be button names or a page's welcome message, and *Open Text* gives descriptive titles to indicate the type of hit.

www.excite.com

altavista.digital.com

nln.com

guide.infoseek.com

www.100hot.com

www.yahoo.com

www.lycos.com

Try Several Search Tools

Try as many different search tools as possible and judge the results for yourself. Speed of access, ease of use, and quality of output will soon help you determine your preferred search tools.

It is also worth trying a search tool such as the *Metacrawler Parallel Web Search Service*. This directs your queries to nine of the leading Web search engines (including *Lycos, Yahoo!*, and *AltaVista*). You can access *Metacrawler* at **http://www. metacrawler.com**.

SEARCHING BY CATEGORY

Most Web-based search engines and directories enable you to search through predefined categories. This can be invaluable if you are browsing for information in one general area. You can also use this method to narrow your search, since there is usually a "search only in this area" option. The example on this page shows how to use the categories option in the *Yahoo!* directory to run a search only in those Web sites devoted to movie quotes. *Yahoo!* can be found at **http://www.yahoo.com**.

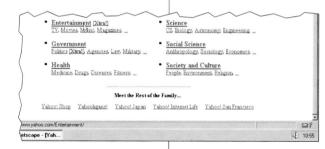

1 On the main *Yahoo!* page, use the scroll bar on the right-hand side of the window to scroll to the bottom of the window. Click *Entertainment*. A new page appears, showing subdivisions of this category.

2 Click on *Movies and Films*. The window displays subdivisions of the *Movies and Films* category. Click on *Quotes*.

3 Type your search term (in this case, **Macbeth**) in the search box at the top of the page, check the *Search only in Quotes* box, then click the *Search* button. A list of URLs will appear in the usual way.

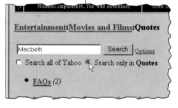

Advanced Searches

When you are using a Web-based search engine, you will often find that a simple one-word description will result in too broad a selection of Web sites. Fortunately, many of these tools have advanced search facilities that allow you to enter more detailed criteria. Most enable you to use simple terms such as "and," "or," and "not" to make a search based on more than one keyword. For example, it would be possible for you to select all sites that mention "guitars" and "amplifiers," while excluding those that mention "bass." Some tools also allow more detailed search parameters. Read any available "help" files to see which parameters are permitted at that site for more advanced searches.

USING SEARCH OPERATORS

One of the most commonly recognized special characters for narrowing the range of "hits" is the quotation mark. If you want to search for sites on the Rolling Stones and type **Rolling Stones** as your search term you will probably get a list of pages that contain either word. By placing the search term in quotation marks your search tool should only list pages containing the phrase "Rolling Stones."

The sequence in which they appear is usually controlled by a "relevance" measurement, normally shown as a percentage figure. On very generalized searches, those with a high percentage of relevance – the ones whose search criteria have been most successfully fulfilled – appear at the top of the list.

The steps on this page show how to use *AltaVista*'s "Advanced Search" feature to search for Web pages that feature both the Beatles and the Rolling Stones. First connect to *AltaVista*'s site, then follow these steps:

Commonly Used Search Operators

Search operators differ between the various search engines and directories, so it's always a good idea to consult the "help" or "tips" screens to see which ones work. Here is a list of some of the more commonly used operators:

- **""** — Quotation marks are used for search criteria involving more than one element – such as a phrase or sentence.

- **and** — Links together any number of key words (sometimes replaceable by **+**).

- **or** — Searches using one set of criteria or another, when there are two or more search terms.

- **near** — Placed between two search terms, this finds pages where the search terms are close together (perhaps ten words apart) in the document.

- ***** — In some tools, asterisks can be used for "wild-card" searches. For example, **typ*** will find "type," "typist," "typical," "typhoid," etc.

- *x* **but not** *y* — Searches for specific criteria but excluding others (sometimes replaceable by **-**).

1 Click the *Advanced* search button on the home page for *AltaVista*.

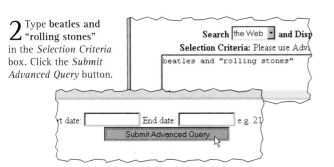

2 Type beatles and "rolling stones" in the *Selection Criteria* box. Click the *Submit Advanced Query* button.

3 A new page appears, listing the first ten entries that fulfil your search criteria.

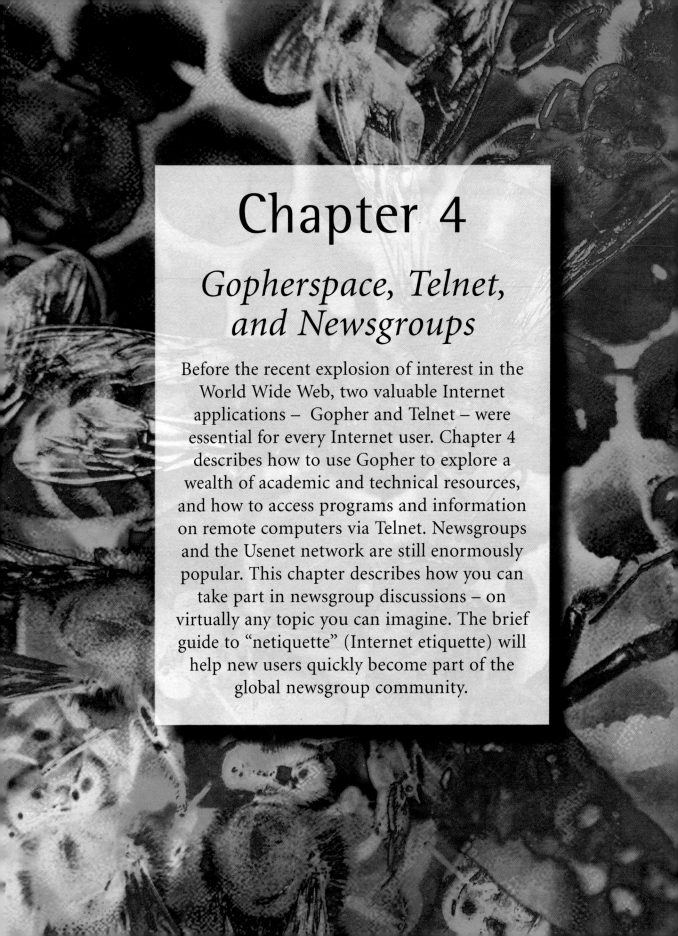

Chapter 4

Gopherspace, Telnet, and Newsgroups

Before the recent explosion of interest in the World Wide Web, two valuable Internet applications – Gopher and Telnet – were essential for every Internet user. Chapter 4 describes how to use Gopher to explore a wealth of academic and technical resources, and how to access programs and information on remote computers via Telnet. Newsgroups and the Usenet network are still enormously popular. This chapter describes how you can take part in newsgroup discussions – on virtually any topic you can imagine. The brief guide to "netiquette" (Internet etiquette) will help new users quickly become part of the global newsgroup community.

4

Using Gopher

GOPHER IS ONE OF THE INFORMATION RETRIEVAL SYSTEMS on the Internet that predates the World Wide Web. Developed in 1991 at the University of Minnesota, it was the first system that enabled you to leap invisibly from site to site simply by choosing a menu option on the page. For this reason it became more popular than many of its counterparts, superseded finally by the arrival of the Web. Gopher gives you access to a vast number of servers world-wide. Most of these are maintained by universities or government bodies, and they have information on a wide range of subjects, much of which is specialized and unlikely to be available on Web sites. Gopher servers, like FTP servers, hold files and documents that you can view on-line or transfer to your PC.

Where Can I Find a Gopher Client?
The original home of Gopher, the University of Minnesota, has an FTP site that has most Gopher client software available for you to download using anonymous FTP (see page 42). You can connect to this site at: **boombox.micro.umn.edu/pub/gopher**.

How Does Gopherspace Work?

Just as all the Web sites around the world make up the World Wide Web, the world's 5,000 or more Gopher servers are collectively known as "Gopherspace." In many ways, accessing a Gopher server is similar to using an FTP site, in that information is presented in menus containing files and folders. In Gopherspace these folders are known as "Gopher holes." You navigate through the holes to find files, documents, or further holes containing yet more levels of information. You can usually view or download the files that you find simply by clicking on them.

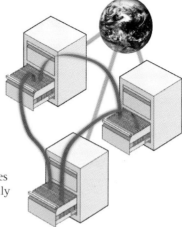

CONNECTING TO GOPHER VIA THE WEB
When Gopher first appeared, you could only access it using a Gopher client program. Nowadays, most users access Gopher sites from a Web browser. The main advantage of using Gopher software is that it usually comes with a built-in list of Gopher addresses. However, every Gopher server provides at least one link to other Gopher servers, so this is not a serious hindrance to using a browser. For example, try connecting to one of the sites listed on this page (remember to prefix the URL with **gopher://** instead of **http://**), and then bookmark that site. Now you can access other Gopher servers easily from the Web.

OTHER GOPHER SERVERS
The examples below show how to use the Gopher Menu to find links to other servers and how to search Gopherspace.

Gopher Servers

A typical Gopher server contains a wide variety of information, from periodicals and academic research papers to details about the weather. The list below gives a few example Gopher sites. (If you are using a Web browser, remember to prefix each address with **gopher://**.)

❑ **University of Southern California**
Includes information on anthropology, sports, archaeology, economics, and business.
cwis.usc.edu

❑ **University of Minnesota**
Contains Gopher holes devoted to fun and games, and discussion groups. It also provides links to many other Gopher servers.
gopher.micro.umn.edu

❑ **Wiretap Gopher**
Access to US and world government document archives, searchable on-line libraries, and electronic books.
wiretap.spies.com

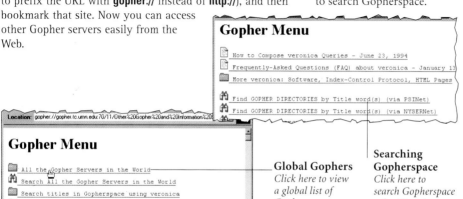

Gopher Menu

How to Compose veronica Queries – June 23, 1994
Frequently-Asked Questions (FAQ) about veronica – January 13
More veronica: Software, Index-Control Protocol, HTML Pages
Find GOPHER DIRECTORIES by Title word(s) (via PSINet)
Find GOPHER DIRECTORIES by Title word(s) (via NYSERNet)

Location: gopher://gopher.tc.umn.edu:70/11/Other%20Gopher%20and%20Information%20...

Gopher Menu

All the Gopher Servers in the World
Search All the Gopher Servers in the World
Search titles in Gopherspace using veronica

Global Gophers
Click here to view a global list of Gopher servers.

Searching Gopherspace
Click here to search Gopherspace using Veronica.

Searching Through Gopherspace

Gopher really comes into its own if you have specific information that you want to find. As with other Internet retrieval systems, the best way to go about this is to perform a search. It is possible to search all of Gopherspace using special search tools called Veronica and Jughead. You can run a Veronica search from most Gopher servers. Veronica will search a wide range of files, including text files, images, and programs. It can also retrieve articles from newsgroups. Clicking on the Veronica hole of a Gopher menu will bring up another menu with files and FAQs about Veronica and several search options. For example, you can usually search for keywords that appear in directory titles, or make a wider search that also covers individual file names. The steps on this page show how you can perform a Veronica search from a Web browser.

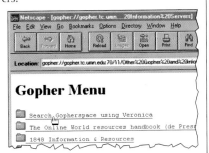

1 First connect to a Gopher site by typing **gopher://** followed by the name of a Gopher site in your browser's location box. Press the Return key. Then click the Veronica entry in the Gopher Menu that appears.

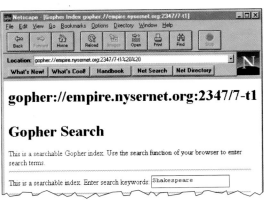

2 On the *Gopher Search* page, type your search term in the *keywords* box and press the Return key.

3 When the list of hits appears, click any line to move to the appropriate file or link on that Gopher site.

Wide Area Information Server

One limitation of using Veronica is that searches are only made on directory or document names, not on their contents. Using a Wide Area Information Server (WAIS), however, you can search the detailed contents of more than 1,000 special databases. The principal drawback of this system is that only WAIS-readable databases can be accessed, which means that its usefulness is restricted to whether a database covering your own interests has been created. As with Veronica searches, the most straightforward way to perform a WAIS search is via a Gopher menu. Look for the entry "WAIS Based Information" or something similar. After submitting your query in a search box, you will see a list of hits in a Gopher menu. You can also access numerous WAIS servers directly via the Web (for example, at **http://www.wais.com**).

Read the Instructions!
When you log on to a Telnet site, read the instructions in the opening menu screens carefully. Like bulletin board services (see page 25), Telnet sites are not all organized in the same way. You can usually call up a help menu by typing **H** or **?** or **help** at any time. If you are really stuck, type **exit** or **logout** to end the session.

Logging on with Telnet

T ELNET – ONE OF THE OLDEST INTERNET ACTIVITIES – allows you to log on to a remote computer from your PC and access services there. In a Telnet session, you actually run programs on the remote computer as though you were sitting at it. Most people use Telnet to access on-line databases, or to read articles and books on-line, although it is also possible to run other programs at the remote site. You can also use Telnet to play on-line games, such as chess, with other users who are logged on to that site. As with FTP, you can log on to many Telnet sites as a guest user. Some universities, libraries, and research organizations offer free Telnet access, although not all Telnet sites are free. Many commercial organizations require you to register and pay a fee to use their services.

How Does Telnet Work?

Using Telnet is a little like using an old-fashioned terminal at a public library. You control the session from your keyboard, choosing options from a list and typing a number or letter to access a series of menu screens. You navigate through the system on the remote Telnet computer in much the same way as you do in a BBS session (see page 25). You may find it difficult to save the information you see on screen to your hard disk. Some Telnet programs only allow you to save a screen of information at a time to your hard disk.

Typical Telnet Screens

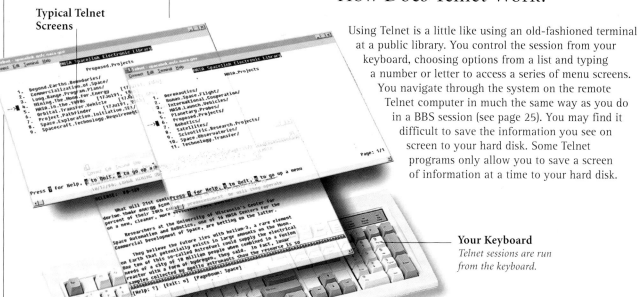

Your Keyboard
Telnet sessions are run from the keyboard.

USING TELNET
Telnet lets you log on to a remote computer to access a wide range of services. These example pages are from NASA's Spacelink site at **spacelink.msfc.nasa.gov***. See the steps opposite for how to connect to this and other Telnet sites.*

Some Web Sites with Links to Telnet Sites

❑ **http://www.orion.org/internet_services/telnet.html**

The Orion Online Network has a list of scientific, sports, and educational Telnet sites. When you click on this page's links to Telnet sites, your Telnet client should launch automatically (see box opposite).

❑ **http://honor.uc.wlu.edu/tenet.html**

This site has hot links to hundreds of Telnet resources, and even has a search facility to help you find sites that interest you.

Running a Telnet Session

There are two main ways to use Telnet. For both you need Telnet software. A Telnet client is supplied with *Windows 95*, or you can download one from an Internet software site, such as **http://www.windows95.com**. If you have difficulty finding the *Windows 95* Telnet client on your hard disk, see the tip box below. The steps on this page show you how to use the *Windows 95* Telnet client to log on to a Telnet site. First double-click the *Telnet* icon in the *Windows* folder, then follow these steps.

1 Choose *Remote System* from the *Connect* menu. The *Connect* box will pop up.

2 Type the name of a site you wish to access in the *Host Name* panel of the *Connect* box, then click the *Connect* button. When you have connected to the site, a login screen will appear.

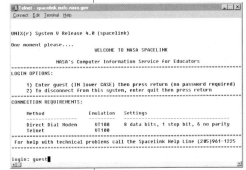

3 Once you are connected, follow the on-screen instructions. In this example type **guest** for your login name, as specified, and press the Return key. Follow subsequent instructions to access further information.

Telnet via a Web Browser

It is possible to access Telnet sites from the Web by configuring your browser to access a Telnet program, and replacing **http://** with **telnet://** before the site's address. To configure *Netscape Navigator*, follow the steps below. The next time you access a Telnet site, the Telnet client will be launched automatically.

1 From the *Options* menu in the main *Navigator* window, choose *General Preferences*. The *Preferences* dialog box will appear.

2 On the *Apps* page, click the *Browse* button next to the *Telnet Application* box and then navigate to your Telnet program in the *Select a Telnet Application* window. Click on the Telnet application and choose *Open*.

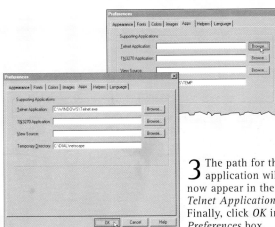

3 The path for this application will now appear in the *Telnet Application* box. Finally, click *OK* in the *Preferences* box.

Can't Find the Windows 95 Telnet Program?

The *Windows 95* Telnet client does not appear on the *Start* menu. To locate it, access the Find utility from your *Start* menu, choose *Files or Folders*, type **Telnet** in the *Named* box and click *OK*. Right-click the Telnet application icon when it appears, and drag it onto the desktop. Release the mouse button over the desktop and choose *Create Shortcut(s) Here* from the menu that appears.

Newsgroups on the Internet

NEWSGROUPS ON THE INTERNET HAVE VERY LITTLE TO DO WITH "NEWS," but everything to do with discussion and debate. Newsgroups are essentially public e-mail discussion forums: participants "post" messages to be seen by all readers of the newsgroup. Anyone reading these messages can choose either to reply publicly (by posting a follow-up message to the newsgroup) or privately (by sending the author a private e-mail message). Newsgroups provide a forum for interested parties to "discuss" topics of mutual interest. As with e-mail messages, it is possible to include encoded sounds, images, or videoclips in newsgroup postings. Newsgroups offer some of the most stimulating, useful, and controversial content on the Internet, depending on which groups you are looking at (see opposite for some examples).

How Do Mailing Lists Differ from Newsgroups?
Both newsgroups and mailing lists (see page 54) offer forums for discussion on the Internet, but they operate in different ways. Messages posted to a newsgroup can be viewed by all users (as long as their service provider supplies that newsgroup). Mailing lists relay all group messages directly to your mailbox, so unless you actively subscribe to a list you will not be able to browse its contents.

The Usenet Network

Usenet (an abbreviation of User's Network) is not a computer network in the physical sense. It is a vast body of newsgroups that are distributed around the world by computers called "news servers." These news servers exchange information so that each one carries a copy of the most recent messages. Usenet is not actually part of the Internet, although many Internet sites are used to carry and distribute its newsgroups. Computers that are not linked to the Internet can also access newsgroups, for example, by dialing a bulletin board system that carries Usenet messages.

NEWSGROUP MESSAGES
A newsgroup is similar in some ways to a public noticeboard where people post, read, or reply to messages. Newsgroups provide thousands of these "noticeboards" – each devoted to a specific subject.

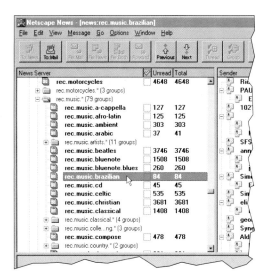

NETSCAPE NEWSREADER
The *Netscape Navigator* Web browser has a built-in newsreader that provides easy access to the Usenet newsgroups. Be aware, however, that your provider may not supply you with all the available newsgroups (see tip box on page 88).

Origins of Usenet

Usenet was first conceived in 1979 when Tom Truscott and Jim Ellis, two postgraduate students at Duke University, North Carolina, wrote some "news" software and installed it on two Unix computers. This software allowed them to post messages across a network that both machines could access. In 1982 the software was released publicly. As the number of users increased, it became more helpful for messages to be organized according to their subject matter. From there the newsgroup concept evolved. Although it is hard to estimate accurately the number of newsgroups, there are now thought to be between 16,000 and 20,000.

Newsgroup Classifications

Usenet newsgroups are divided into about 20 major subject classifications, known as top-level categories. Other top-level categories also exist, for newsgroups concerned with specific countries, for example. Here are some of the main subject classifications, with a few groups as examples:

NEWS (OVER **20** GROUPS)
Groups concerned with the News network – useful software, new groups, help with Usenet. If you're new to Usenet, look here first:
news.announce.newusers
news.newusers. questions

COMP (OVER **750** GROUPS)
Computer-oriented groups – computer marketplaces, technical advice, and game hints are all available here.
comp.sys.ibm.pc.games.adventure

ALT (OVER **2,500** GROUPS)
"Alternative" groups – from independent music to New Age remedies. Alt groups often post pictures and sounds.
alt.astrology
alt.music.beatles

MISC (OVER **100** GROUPS)
Newsgroups not easy to classify – from bodybuilding to pension funds.
misc.invest.stocks
misc.education.multimedia

BIZ (OVER **60** GROUPS)
Business groups – where marketing and advertising are acceptable activities.
biz.jobs.offered

REC (OVER **550** GROUPS)
Groups devoted to recreational activities. This classification covers most of the arts.
rec.sport.triathlon
rec.travel.africa

TALK (OVER **20** GROUPS)
Debate-oriented forums on any topic, particularly the more controversial ones.
talk.euthanasia

SOC (OVER **200** GROUPS)
Groups concerned with social issues – from the environment and politics to socializing.
soc.rights.human

SCI (OVER **150** GROUPS)
Groups interested in scientific debate, and in research and development.
sci.virtual-worlds
sci.med.diseases.cancer

Newsgroups Outside Usenet
Some newsgroups do exist outside the Usenet umbrella, but they are usually devoted to local issues. For example, some service providers supply one or more newsgroups of their own in addition to the Usenet groups. Such newsgroups are often set up locally by the provider to allow subscribers to share information about the service. These newsgroups are not necessarily distributed to other news servers.

How Are Newsgroups Organized?

Like standard URLs or e-mail addresses, newsgroups have distinctive names that follow a hierarchical structure. The **rec** prefix in this example indicates that this group deals with recreational matters. The **rec** group contains hundreds of subjects, such as art, sports, and music.

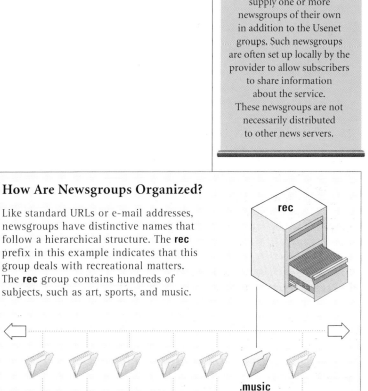

rec

.music

Sublevels
As you move down from the top-level hierarchy, each group contains multiple subgroups. These subgroups are separated by a point in the newsgroup name.

.makers

Rec.music.makers.guitar
This newsgroup is one of many within the **rec.music.makers** *subgroup. The arrows in this diagram indicate that there are likely to be more newsgroups within every subgroup.*

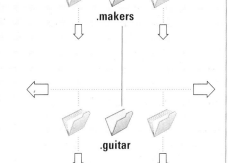

.guitar

How to Behave in Newsgroups

Usenet is not an officially organized body, so there are no hard-and-fast rules to dictate the behavior of its members. However, a voluntary code of ethics has grown up with the network. Usenet has been around for years, predating the Internet itself, and many of its regular users become exasperated by "newbies" who barge into discussions without having done any background research about the group. For example, some newbies post totally irrelevant questions because they haven't bothered to find out if a group is concerned with their particular query. They may also ask basic questions that regulars can get tired of answering repeatedly. Maintaining an awareness of other members of Usenet and their needs should help your first discussions to be enjoyable experiences. Also bear in mind the more general forms of "netiquette" (see opposite).

WHERE TO BEGIN

With almost 20,000 newsgroups to choose from, there is certain to be something that caters for every possible interest. Browsing the Usenet group **news.lists** will give you an up-to-date picture of the Usenet scene. Among the first groups you should look at are **news.announce.newusers** and **news.newusers.questions**. Both these newsgroups were specifically created to help newbies successfully walk the tightrope of newsgroup netiquette.

Why Are Some Newsgroups Unavailable?
Usenet has such a huge number of newsgroups that Internet providers are often unable to dedicate enough space on their servers to carry them all. Consequently, many providers carry only a selected number of groups (some deliberately exclude "nonfamily" groups). If you find that yours doesn't carry a particular group, you could try asking the service administrator to get it; many will be happy to oblige.

Useful Guidelines

When you first start posting to newsgroups you should avoid making comments that might incur the wrath of other users. Remembering the following general points (also see opposite page) may save you from any unnecessary embarrassment.

Lurking

Before you make your first posting to a newsgroup, "lurk" in the group for a few days. To lurk is to observe the discussions of a group without joining in. In spite of the implications of the term, this is an acceptable, even sensible, practice. It allows you to find out what a group is concerned with, if it interests you, and the level at which any potential posting should be pitched. Lurking can also let you build up knowledge of a subject without actively having to participate in that newsgroup. For example, you may be interested in the discussions of a group, but have nothing to contribute yourself.

Don't Quote Me

It is common sense not to believe everything you read in a newspaper. This advice is even more important when dealing with newsgroups. While the media has a responsibility to maintain a certain degree of accuracy, the same is not true of newsgroups. Any newsgroup you join is likely to contain as wide a mix of people and personalities as you would find walking down a crowded street. The people posting their advice and opinions may range from the expert to the downright deranged. It's up to you to sort out what's fact and what's fiction.

NATIONAL EXPOSE
ELVIS SPOTTED IN CYBERSPACE

A Brief Guide to Newsgroup "Netiquette"

Read the FAQ
Many newsgroups, particularly those of a technical nature, have a FAQ (a document containing Frequently Asked Questions) that new members can consult. Reading this might help solve a problem without your having to trouble the group with a basic question.

Be Relevant
Some users of newsgroups can at times be intolerant of the behavior of new members. Because newsgroups often deal with a narrow range of issues, ensure that your message is relevant to the group before you post it.

Be Descriptive
Give your posting a descriptive title. Not everyone will be concerned with what you have to say, so it's a little unkind to expect other members to read a complete article just to find out about its contents.

Be Brief
Try to keep your posting as concise as possible. Write in a clear, succinct manner, avoiding the temptation to show off your vocabulary.

Be Careful with Humor
With written forms of communication, it can sometimes be difficult to project humor or irony. If you make a remark that is ambiguous in its tone, it's a good idea to back it up with an "emoticon" (see page 99), although some people staunchly refuse to use these symbols.

Following Up
If someone has asked a simple question, there is a good chance that many people will respond. You should post a response to the group only if you think your answer is of wider interest; otherwise, send a personal e-mail to the author. Note that if the original message was posted to several newsgroups, your newsreader may attempt to post your reply to the same ones. If your reply is not relevant to them all, remove the irrelevant addresses before you post.

Don't Advertise in the Wrong Group
You may think that a newsgroup provides you with a captive audience, but nothing provokes collective anger more than the posting of a hard-sell advertisement. There are accepted places and ways to advertise in Usenet, such as newsgroups with "marketplace" or "biz" in their name.

Avoid Spamming
"Spamming" – posting identical messages to many different newsgroups – is considered to be the height of impoliteness, and groups have their own way of "policing" such misdemeanors. Spammers may suddenly find themselves "mail-bombed" by thousands of pieces of junk e-mail that can render their account unusable or take days to download.

Try Not to Be Rude
If you feel angered by a posting, you might consider sending a private e-mail rather than conducting an argument in public. Remember, thousands of other users will be able to follow it up if you post to the whole newsgroup. If you are actively looking for confrontation, there are newsgroups that specialize in nothing else – for example, **alt.flame**.

Reading Newsgroups

There are many different programs with which you can read newsgroups. You can even read them through a Web browser. However, the dedicated newsreaders tend to have better features for following discussions and are generally more flexible. Many good freeware newsreaders are available on the Internet and it is worth trying out a few to see which one suits you best. Essentially, they all perform the same task, but some have more features than others and they present information in different ways. Whichever program you choose, you will need to provide some information about your Internet account, such as the names of your news and mail servers, and personal details (see example below).

Off-Line Newsreaders
When choosing a newsreader, you may want to consider whether or not it allows you to read off-line. An off-line newsreader will reduce your phone bill considerably by keeping on-line connection time to a minimum. It connects only to retrieve or send information. At other times you read downloaded messages or compose replies off-line.

1 Double-click the *Agent* icon to start the *Free Agent* newsreader.

SETTING UP FREE AGENT

Free Agent is one of the more comprehensive newsreading programs available, packed with features that allow you a high degree of flexibility in managing your newsgroups. The program is available as shareware or freeware; the freeware version can be found at **http://www.webpress.net/ forte/agent/index.htm**. *Free Agent* will be downloaded as a compressed file which you will need to expand before you can run it (see Appendix 3). Once you have done this, connect to your service provider and follow these steps to set up the program on your computer.

2 The *Free Agent Setup* dialog box appears. Type the name of your news server in the *News (NNTP) Server* box, and the name of your mail server in the *Mail (SMTP) Server* box. Your service provider should tell you this information. If you don't know it, refer to the checklist on page 33 or check their documentation (if any). Type your e-mail address in the *Email Address* box.

3 Click on the arrow to the right of the *Time Zone* box and choose the correct zone for your town or city from the drop-down menu. Finally, click OK.

4 A dialog box appears, asking if you want to go on-line now. Click *Yes* to download a list of the newsgroups carried by your provider. (This may take a while.)

5 Once *Free Agent* has downloaded the full list of newsgroups, they will appear in the *All Groups* panel. Use the scroll bar on the right to browse the list.

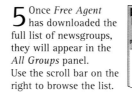

OPENING A MESSAGE AND FOLLOWING A THREAD

Some newsreaders allow you to follow "threads." A thread is a series of messages that make up a discussion on a particular subject. A newsreader that supports threads displays messages in chronological order so that you can follow a discussion easily without having to hunt through a long list of articles to find the next related posting. The steps below show you how to follow a thread using *Free Agent*.

What Does Subscribe Mean?

Subscribing to a newsgroup simply means identifying a particular group as being one that you are interested in following, and instructing your newsreader to remember its name. However, you will not necessarily receive messages automatically. The groups may just be sectioned off to make them easier to find, or tagged so that you can download new messages for all your subscribed newsgroups at once.

1 In the *All Groups* panel, double-click the name of the group you want to read.

2 The *View Empty Group* dialog box appears, with a choice of viewing options. In this example click the *Sample 50 Article Headers* button. The first fifty article titles in that group will then be downloaded and displayed in the *Subject* window.

3 Messages that start a thread are marked by an arrow to the left of the message header. To open a thread and view the full list of messages related to it, click this arrow.

4 To open a specific message in the thread, select it in the right-hand panel and press Return. The message text will appear in the bottom panel.

5 Subsequent messages in the thread can be viewed chronologically by clicking the *View Next Unread Article in Thread* button. Repeat this step for each new message you want to read.

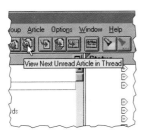

Other Popular Newsreading Programs

❑ **WinVN**

Freeware. You can only use it on-line. It has limited features (for example, you can't mark articles in advance for retrieval), but it is simple and user-friendly. You can find it at **ftp.ksc.nasa.gov/pub/winvn/Win95/**.

❑ **News Xpress**

Freeware. Can be used on-line and off-line. Provides good features for handling threads and marking articles. You can download it from the following FTP site: **ftp.hk.super.net/pub/windows/Winsock-1-Utilities/Windows95/News/**.

Posting to Newsgroups

Once you have come to grips with the basic features of your newsreader and can navigate your way successfully through the various newsgroups and messages, you will probably want to be more adventurous. You may want to participate in a group by posting your own messages, or to download files with image, audio, or video attachments (see the steps on these pages). You may also want to explore the more complex features of your newsreader. For example, it is possible to configure some programs so that they filter information. This means that you could opt not to receive messages or newsgroups that have certain words in their titles. Some programs even allow you to block messages from people you find annoying. If you want to experiment, try referring to your newsreader's "help" file.

POSTING MESSAGES WITH A NEWSREADER

There are more ways than one to post messages to a newsgroup. You can initiate a new discussion, you can reply publicly to a message that's been posted by someone else, or you can reply directly by e-mail to the person who posted the original message. Most newsreaders enable you to follow up a posting and send e-mail. The steps on this page show how to use *Free Agent* to follow up a newsgroup message that you are currently reading. First, repeat Steps 1, 2, and 4 on page 91, then follow the steps on this page.

1 Click the *Post Follow Up Article* button. A mail window will appear with the text of the original message included and the address of the group already in place.

2 Type the address of the person whose message you are responding to in the *Email To* box. The name will appear at the top of the *Text* box. (It is considered "polite" to reply personally as well as publicly.)

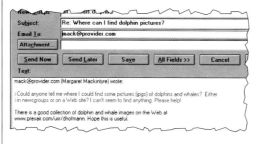

3 Edit the original message, if necessary, so that it only includes the points you are responding to. Type your follow-up message in the *Text* window.

4 When you have finished, click the *Send Now* button. The message will be posted to the newsgroup and an e-mail will be sent to the author of the original message.

ATTACHING AND DECODING BINARY FILES

Messages posted to newsgroups can have binary attachments in the form of sound, image, and video files, as well as program applications. Groups that carry binary files usually have "binaries" in their name – **alt.binaries.pictures.gardens**, for example. Before a binary file can be posted in a message, it has to be encoded. Similarly, you will have to decode any binary that you download from a newsgroup before you can view it. Some newsreaders have a built-in facility for decoding binary attachments. The example on this page shows how to decode a binary attachment using *Free Agent* while on-line. First open a newsgroup containing binary attachments (in this example, **alt.binaries.pictures.astro**), then follow the steps below.

1 Click on the file you wish to view in the right-hand panel of the main *Free Agent* window.

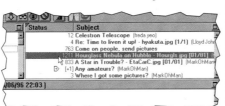

2 Right-click on the highlighted file name and choose *Launch Binary Attachments* from the drop-down menu.

Make Sure You Have the Right Viewers
You must have a suitable program installed for handling files that you download. For example, you may find your newsreader doesn't display automatically the image file at Step 3 below. In this case you need to install a graphics program on your PC. *Paint Shop Pro* is a popular program that can handle most image formats. It is available as shareware from many Internet sites, including **http://www.windows95.com**.

3 After the data has transferred, the image should appear in a new window. The newsreader does this by running the appropriate graphics application on your PC. (See the tip box on this page if the image does not appear automatically.)

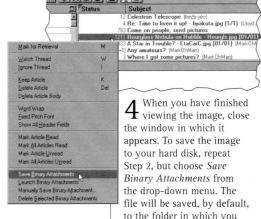

Handling Multipart Binary Files

Many files posted to "binaries" newsgroups (especially large multimedia files) are split into a series of smaller files. If a message comprises an image file in six parts, you will need to download all six parts – identified as (01/06), (02/06), and so on – before you can view the image. Sometimes you may find that part of a multipart file is missing. This might occur for a number of reasons – for example, the sender may have made an error, or the message may have been deleted from the server. If parts of a message are missing, it is not worth downloading any of it.

MESSAGE HEADERS
Headers (this one is taken from Step 1 above) identify the file's name and type.

Number of Parts

Hourglass Nebula on Hubble - hourgls.jpg (01/01)

File Description   **File Name**   **File Type**

4 When you have finished viewing the image, close the window in which it appears. To save the image to your hard disk, repeat Step 2, but choose *Save Binary Attachments* from the drop-down menu. The file will be saved, by default, to the folder in which you installed *Free Agent*.

93

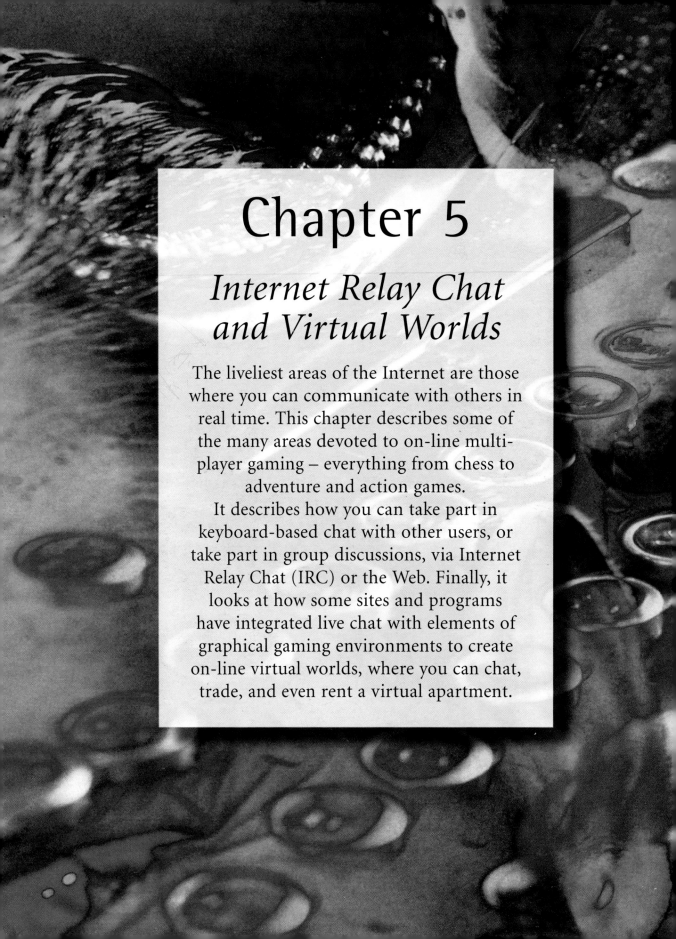

Chapter 5

Internet Relay Chat and Virtual Worlds

The liveliest areas of the Internet are those where you can communicate with others in real time. This chapter describes some of the many areas devoted to on-line multi-player gaming – everything from chess to adventure and action games.

It describes how you can take part in keyboard-based chat with other users, or take part in group discussions, via Internet Relay Chat (IRC) or the Web. Finally, it looks at how some sites and programs have integrated live chat with elements of graphical gaming environments to create on-line virtual worlds, where you can chat, trade, and even rent a virtual apartment.

5

Playing On-Line Games

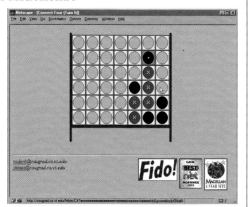

For the computer games player, the Net provides a treasure house of gaming resources – new software to download, upgrades and add-ons for commercial games software, newsgroups and Web sites full of hints, tips, and cheats for your favorite games. But the most exciting aspect of the Internet for gamers is the opportunity to play against other players in one-on-one or multiplayer modem games. As you read this, thousands of people are playing Net games. These pages give a flavor of some of the games currently in progress.

Playing Against a Computer

You will find many different types of games on the Web. Usually you need no software other than your Web browser to play them on-line. You simply access the Web page and follow any instructions on-screen. You can play a wide range of games – from chess to trivia quizzes to simple adventure games – against a computer. For many games you will need extra Web browser plug-ins, such as Macromedia's *Shockwave.* Many versions of arcade-type games such as *Space Invaders, Frogger,* and *Tetris* have been adapted for the Internet. The illustrations on the right show examples of two popular Web-based games.

CONNECT FOUR
You can find a version of the popular *Connect Four* game on the Web at **http://csugrad.cs.vt.edu/htbin/connect4.perl**. This version, by Joe Hines and Brian Roder, does not require Web browser plug-in software.

NEURO GOLF
Neurotec's *Neuro Golf* (a cross between crazy golf and pinball) requires the *Shockwave for Director* plug-in. You can play a round either against the computer or a friend sitting at your PC. You can even create and use your own course. This site is at **http://www.neurotec.com/demos/shockwav/neurogolf.html**.

Where Do I Find Them?
The easiest way to find the latest games sites is to run a search for "computer games" or "online games" using your favorite Web-based search tool. This will provide you with sites devoted to on-line gaming or games resources, such as the Games Domain site (**http://www.gamesdomain.com**) and Extreme Communications Inc.'s list of Internet games (**http://www.extreme.ca/cool.htm**).

Playing Games via Telnet

You can use Telnet to access MUDs (Multiuser Dungeons or Dimensions). MUDs predate the Internet by many years (the first was developed at the University of Essex, England, in 1979) and are still enormously popular. They are usually text-based games with the emphasis on role-playing, exploration of an imaginary environment, and problem solving. Combat ("killing" monsters and other on-line players) features highly in some MUDs, while others offer more educational or social environments. The original MUD spawned many variants, such as the MUSH (Multiuser Shared Hallucination) and TinyMUD, both of which are more social by nature. People often visit a MUSH simply to chat in a sometimes bizarre on-line world. If you are intrigued and want to know more, look for the FAQs in the **rec.games.mud** newsgroup, or visit the Index of the MUD Resource Collection at **http://www.cis.upenn.edu/~lwl/mudinfo.html**.

Playing Head-to-Head

Microsoft's *Internet Gaming Zone* is a good example of a site where you can play games in real time over the Internet with anyone else who is logged on at that time. You must first download the software (from **http://igz2.microsoft.com**), and then complete a very simple registration form for a user name and password. Once logged on, you arrive at a "village" (see right) where you can choose from a number of buildings – each devoted to a different game. Inside each building is an area where you can chat with other users, view games in progress, or begin a game. You will usually see requests for opponents in the chat area.

The Village
By double-clicking on the building of your choice in the Village area you enter a room devoted to a particular game, such as chess, bridge, checkers, hearts, or reversi.

Checkers
Once inside the game, simply drag and drop your pieces to make your moves. You can also chat with your opponent by typing in the box at the bottom of the window.

In a Games Room
To begin a game, double-click an empty seat. View a game in progress by double-clicking an occupied seat.

Multiplayer Games

Many leading games companies, such as Origin Systems, Sierra On-line, and Virgin Interactive Entertainment, use the World Wide Web to test their latest games. Such sites can provide excellent on-line games for Net users. Usually all you need to do is download and register the software (this may be more than 10 MB so make sure you read the game's description first). You will then be sent a password to enter the game. This example shows *Meridian 59*, a multiplayer, on-line adventure game available at **http://www.3do.com**.

3DO'S MERIDIAN 59
Meridian 59 is a role-playing adventure game. In this on-line 3-D world, you can explore, trade items, interact with other players, and do battle with various enemies – both monsters and other players. You can play alone or join one of the various "guilds" of players.

Your Alter Ego
When you begin the game you choose your character's appearance. This is how you will be seen by other players.

The Game Window
The left-hand side of the window shows the main game screen. You use the cursor keys to move around the environment. You "speak" to other players via the chat box at the bottom of the window. The right-hand side of the window shows your status, health, and inventory.

Talking "Live" on the Internet

L IVE "CHAT," LIKE E-MAIL AND NEWSGROUPS, LETS YOU COMMUNICATE with people from all over the world, but in real time. There are many ways to chat with other Internet users from your keyboard. You can use a large number of sites on the Web, customized facilities in the on-line services, or connect to Telnet sites devoted to chat. You can also use client software to access one of the networks that host Internet Relay Chat (IRC). This section introduces you to the concept of live chatting by explaining how to set up an IRC client program, how to configure it to access an IRC server, and how to begin a conversation. It will also look at some Web sites devoted to live chat that are good starting points for beginners.

Internet Relay Chat

Internet Relay Chat is a multiuser chat system that allows many people to communicate simultaneously across the Internet, in real time. It was developed in Finland by Jarkko Oikarinen, in 1988. IRC conversations take place on "channels" (see opposite) and you "chat" with other people by typing messages at the keyboard. To take part in IRC you need to run a client program on your computer while connected to the Internet (see page 100). Some of the newer IRC programs now also support video and audio conferences as well as keyboard chat.

IRC is organized in networks; there are currently about 15 different networks that exist independently of one another. Each consists of a series of servers that constantly relay chat back and forth among themselves. You access IRC by connecting to one specific server, and this automatically gives you access to that entire network. Your choice of server determines which network you join.

CHOOSING AN IRC NETWORK
As no two networks have the same set of channels available (*#newbies* on Dalnet is not the same channel as *#newbies* on Efnet), you will want to choose one that suits your interests and temperament. Some people relish the noise of the larger networks, EFnet and Undernet, while others prefer a quieter place to talk, like the Star Trek enthusiasts who started up Dalnet. Some networks have specialized interests; the Chiron network in Canada, for example, is dedicated to games chat. Explore the networks to see which you like best.

TALKING ON CHANNELS
The channel system on IRC networks can be compared to the Citizens' Band (CB) radio system – you can only talk to people on the same band or channel as you are, and you can keep switching channels to talk to different people. *CompuServe* has a live chat program that is actually called *CB Simulator*.

Where Do I Begin?
IRC can be daunting to new users because it is fast, dynamic, and appears at first to have a steep learning curve. IRC FAQs and IRC Primers provide useful background information, (you can find them by running a search for "IRC" on the Web). You could also monitor the newsgroups **alt.irc** and **alt.irc.help** for further background information. When you are ready, join the *#newbies* or *#ircnewbies* channels first. These will let you gradually find your feet, without feeling intimidated.

What Are Channels?

Channels are the virtual locations on IRC networks where users meet to talk to one another. The larger networks have thousands of channels, and you have to join one of them before you can talk with other people. It is even possible to have conversations going on several channels at once. Some channels do stipulate a topic of conversation, but others are less rigid and just invite general chat. Even when a topic has been set, it is not always adhered to, and you can suggest a change whenever you like. Channels have different "modes." Most channels are "public," but you can also talk on a "private" or "secret" channel, where it is possible to restrict access, for example, to "invite only."

How Channels Are Run

Every channel is run by an operator. You become the channel operator if you are the first person to join an existing channel that has become empty, or if you create a new one. You can also be made an operator by a person who already has "op" status. Channel operators have special powers in IRC; they can set the channel mode and even control who is allowed on it.

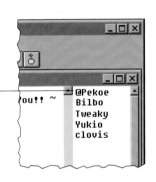

Channel Operators
Channel operators have an @ symbol in front of their name. There is often more than one operator on a channel, particularly if it is busy.

Channel Name
The name of every IRC channel is directly preceded by a # symbol.

Emoticons and Abbreviations

When you start using Internet Relay Chat, you may notice that some messages contain abbreviations and strange punctuation marks known as "emoticons" (emotional icons). These are used to add emotional coloring and emphasis to messages. Acronyms have been adopted as a form of shorthand, to make life easier for people who type slowly. Emoticons can help to reinforce the tone of messages in a text-based medium where misunderstanding is easy. Humor, for example, is very apt to be misinterpreted – especially when you can't hear the "speaker's" tone of voice or see his or her facial expression. Adding an emoticon can let the reader know that you are not being entirely serious. Some examples of acronyms and emoticons are given below. These conventions extend to most discussion areas of the Internet, such as newsgroups and e-mail.

Some Common Emoticons

:-)	Happy	|-O	Yawn
:-))	Very happy	:-|	Hmmph!
;-)	Winking	:-||	Angry
:-7	Wry smile	%-)	Confused
:-D	Laughing out loud	:-X	Not speaking
:-p	Tongue-in-cheek	:-&	Tongue-tied
:-*	Kiss	:-/	Undecided
:-(	Sad	:-@	Screaming
:-((	Very sad	:-U	Shouting
:'-(	Crying	:-0	Shocked

Common Acronyms and Abbreviations

AFAIK *As Far As I Know*	**BTW** *By The Way*	**IMHO** *In My Humble Opinion*	**OIC** *Oh I See*	**THX** *Thanks*
AFK *Away From Keyboard*	**CUL / CUL8R** *See You Later*	**LOL** *Laughing Out Loud*	**ROFL** *Rolling On the Floor Laughing*	**TIA** *Thanks In Advance*
BCNU *Be Seeing You*	**FAQ** *Frequently Asked Questions*	**MORF?** *Male Or Female?*	**RUOK** *Are You OK?*	**WYSIWYG** *What You See Is What You Get*
BRB *Be Right Back*	**IMO** *In My Opinion*	**OAO** *Over And Out*	**SO** *Significant Other*	

Configuring an IRC Client

Most people take part in Internet Relay Chat by using an IRC client program. If your service provider has not supplied an IRC program, you will find many available as freeware or shareware on the Internet. Some of the more popular ones are listed in the box on the opposite page. Before you connect to an IRC server for the first time, you will need to configure your client program. This usually means entering your personal details and the name of an IRC server. The steps on this page show how to configure a client program called *mIRC*. You can download this program from **ftp://papa.indstate.edu/winsoc-I/Windows95/IRC/**.

2 Click the *IRC Servers* tab. Type your name in the *Real Name* box. (You can use an alias here if you prefer.) Type your e-mail address in the *E-Mail* box. Type nicknames in the *Nick Name* and *Alternate* boxes. Finally, click the *Identd* tab.

4 On the *IRC Servers* page, select the name of the server to which you want to connect (see tip box on this page). Finally, click the *Connect* button.

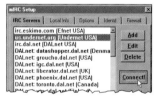

1 First connect to your service provider, then double-click the *Mirc32* icon (in the folder where you installed *mIRC*). The *mIRC Setup* dialog box will appear.

3 On the *Identd* page, check the boxes next to *Enable Identd server* and *Show Identd requests*. Then, in the *User ID* panel, type your user name (usually the part of your e-mail address before the @ symbol). Leave *System* as "Unix," and *Listen on port* as "113." When you have completed this, click the *IRC Servers* tab.

5 In the *mIRC Channels Folder* dialog box, click the name of the channel you want to join (*#ircnewbies* in this example), then click the *Join* button.

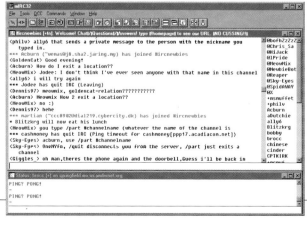

6 The messages for your chosen channel will appear in a new window. You can now chat with other users of this channel by typing your message in the box at the bottom of this window and pressing the Return key.

Running a Session

nce you have configured *mIRC* and joined a channel, he program's main window appears and you are ready to egin your session (see the steps opposite). The illustration low highlights some of the main components of the *mIRC* terface. To find out quickly what any button on the menu ar does, hold the mouse pointer over it. A brief description f the button's function will pop up.

Setup
*Click this to access the
mIRC Setup* dialog box
(see Step 2 opposite).

List Channels
*When you click this button
the* List Channels *dialog box
appears. You can use this to
search for a channel or list
all channels available on the
network you are connected to.*

Disconnect from IRC Server

onnect to IRC Server

Channel Window
*All the messages for a channel
appear in this window. More
than one channel can be open
at a time – each will have its
own separate window.*

tatus Window
*his window tracks activity
n the IRC network. For
xample, it informs you who
as joined or left the network,
nd of any server problems.*

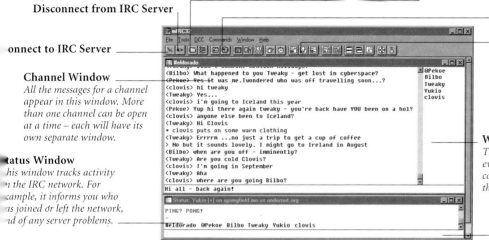

DCC
*Sets up a direct client-
to-client connection.
This means you can talk
directly and exclusively
to one other person.*

Who's Here?
*This panel lists
everybody currently
connected to
this channel.*

Command Lines
*The single line at the
bottom of each window
is where you type your
messages and IRC
commands (see "Basic
IRC Commands").*

ASIC IRC COMMANDS

RC has a long history. When it began, all commands had to e typed at the keyboard. The new generation of IRC clients ow tend to have menu-based interfaces, but most of them till support the traditional keyboard "slash" commands. ere are some of the most basic slash commands that all sers should know, with some examples of how to use them:

help	To get a full list of commands that operate on your IRC server
ist	To view all available channels
quit	To disconnect from the IRC server
oin *[channel]*	To join a channel e.g., /join #newbie
eave *[channel]*	To leave a channel e.g., /leave #newbie
whois *[name]*	To find out more about someone e.g., /whois Brock
nick *[name]*	To change your nick name e.g., /nick TeaFairy
me *[message]*	To describe what you are doing/feeling e.g., /me takes a coffee break
msg *[name] [message]*	To whisper a private message e.g., /msg Pekoe See you next time :-)

Other Popular IRC Programs

❏ **WSIRC**

Shareware. Has person-to-person video conferencing and audio capabilities. There is also a freeware version with fewer features. Available by FTP from **papa.indstate.edu/ winsoc-l/Windows95/IRC/**.

❏ **PIRCH**

Shareware. Has a text-to-speech facility and supports plug-ins like *RealAudio*. You can download it from **http://www.bcpl.lib.md.us/~frappa/**.

❏ **VIRC**

Freeware. *Visual IRC* is a new client for *Windows 95*. It boasts a highly graphic user interface, allowing drag and drop actions to perform many of the basic IRC commands. You can find it at **http://apollo3.com/~acable/**.

Chatting on the Web

The number of live chat sites on the Web is increasing by the month. There are hundreds of sites devoted exclusively to chat, and many now offer chat areas as an additional feature to the site's main content. Some Web pages will provide links to hundreds of chat servers. There are even some programs that you can run in conjunction with your Web browser, so you can share a surfing session on the Web while chatting with a friend (see opposite page).

The seasoned IRC user may find Web-based chat rather slow and cumbersome compared with a session run from an IRC program. Many Web chat sites do not show new messages automatically, and often you need to scroll through several screens before you can pick up the thread of a conversation, making the conversation difficult to follow.

On the positive side, chat on the Web is usually more of a visual experience than it is on IRC. On some sites you can include images and sounds with your messages, and alter their appearance using HTML.

DIFFERENT STYLES OF CHAT

No two Web chat sites are identical, but most share some standard features. Many offer you a choice of places to talk, rather like IRC channels, most require you to provide an identity, and usually you have to update the page manually by clicking a button. The examples below show how some of these features are incorporated into the Globe site (**http://www.theglobe.com**).

Identity
Before you enter a chat area, you need to type a nickname to identify yourself. At the Globe site, you can also choose a "character icon" that will appear next to your name every time you "speak."

Chatting
At many sites you have to update the page regularly by clicking a button. At the Globe site, Listen *updates the messages and* Chat! *sends your message to the site.*

Using HTML
Most chat sites on the Web support HTML. Adding lines of code around your message can make it more eyecatching and help you get "heard" more easily on the page. The code used to produce this message, for example, can be seen in the message window above the Chat! *button.*

FUNCITY CHAT SITE
The Funcity site at **http://www.funcity.com/talk** is an example of a site that really does offer "live" chat on the Web, since the page is updated automatically.

Locating Web Chat Sites

To find details of chat sites on the Web, try running a search for "chat" on one of the Web search engines, or browse the categorized listings of Web sites that some of them provide. Alternatively, try a site like the Web Broadcasting Service (at **http://www.wbs.net**), which has over 100 links to other chat sites on the Web, including chat-related newsgroups.

Web Broadcasting Service
The WBS has its own chat rooms and lists hundreds of good jumping-off points.

SURFING THE WEB WITH NETSCAPE CHAT

You can use some programs, such as *Netscape Chat,* in conjunction with a Web browser to integrate real-time chat with a Web-browsing session. With an IRC channel open in the *Chat* window and a Web page simultaneously open in the *Navigator* window, you can receive Web addresses from other people on the channel: they appear as hot text in the main *Chat* window. Clicking on one will open the relevant page in your browser window. Similarly, you can send the address of any page currently in your browser window to the channel by using the *Send* button (see illustration below). You can even configure this program so that URLs posted to the live channel are displayed by *Navigator* automatically, thereby allowing you to have the same surfing experience as the other people on your channel. *Netscape Chat* is available from **http://home.netscape.com/comprod/chat.html**.

RUNNING NETSCAPE CHAT

When you launch *Netscape Chat, Netscape Navigator* starts automatically if it isn't already running. The illustration below shows how information can be shared between the *Chat* and *Navigator* programs during a chat session.

URL Box
Any URL displayed in Navigator's Location *box also appears in* Chat's URL List *box.*

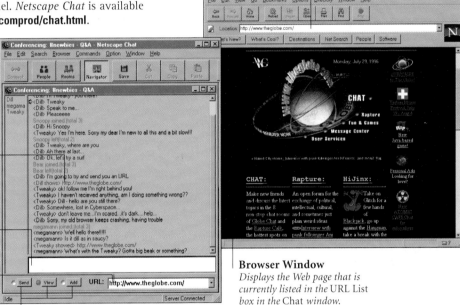

Channel Window
URLs sent by other users appear as blue text in the main chat window. Clicking on a URL will send your browser to that site. The address will also appear in the URL List box.

Speech Box
Type your messages here and press Return to send them to the channel.

URL List Box
You can type URLs here, or navigate to a site using your browser. The URL of any site you visit will appear here automatically.

Send, View, and Add
These buttons apply to the URL displayed in the URL List box. Send displays the URL as a hot link in the channel window; View displays that page in your Web browser; Add adds the URL to your list of sites (you can access this list by clicking the arrow next to the URL List Box).

Browser Window
Displays the Web page that is currently listed in the URL List box in the Chat window.

Talkers

The Web also offers easy access to live "talker" programs that run on Telnet. Like social MUDs (see page 96), talkers have areas devoted purely to chat, usually set in imaginary worlds or locations. Many talker enthusiasts have put together their own Web sites with links to their favorite talkers. If you configure a Telnet program to run with your browser (see page 85), you can access them just by clicking a hot link on one of these Web sites.

Lists of Talkers
You can find this talker list at **http://www.cern.ch/SummerStudents/html/94/talkers.html**.

Exploring Virtual Worlds

SINCE THE END OF 1995, THE WORLD OF ON-LINE CHATTING has gained an exciting new dimension with the arrival of a number of "cyberworlds" or "virtual multiuser environments." These virtual worlds combine elements of on-line chat and graphical adventure games. In early 1996 several such worlds, each with unique characteristics, became available via the World Wide Web or the commercial on-line services. The next few pages will give a flavor of two of these worlds — *Worlds Chat* (from Worlds Inc.) and *WorldsAway* (from Fujitsu Cultural Technologies) — and tell you where to find out more about them.

Where to Find Worlds Chat
You can download the *Worlds Chat Demo* software from the Worlds Inc. site at **http://www.worlds.net**. At this site you will find help files and other information relating to *Worlds Chat*. You can also download software for another virtual world called *AlphaWorld*.

Worlds Chat

The 3-D environment of *Worlds Chat* is based on the concept of a space station that visitors can explore. This space station contains several levels (linked by elevators) and many rooms devoted to different themes. Like most on-line virtual worlds, users are represented by "avatars." An avatar, in this context, is a graphical representation of you that other users can see and interact with. In *Worlds Chat*, you choose your avatar from a selection of portraits hanging on the walls of the Avatar Gallery. You can alter your appearance each time you enter the world. In the free demo version you are simply known as "guest," followed by a number.

CHOOSING AN AVATAR

Once you have downloaded and installed the *Worlds Chat* software, connect to your service provider and start the *Worlds Chat* program (you can access a shortcut via *Windows 95*'s *Start* menu). Follow the steps below to choose an avatar and log on to the *Worlds Chat* server.

1 Using the arrow keys and mouse to navigate, move around the gallery until you have found a suitable image for your avatar, and then click on it. A "walking man" icon will appear in the lower right of the screen and the portrait's frame will become highlighted.

SYSTEM REQUIREMENTS
You need at least a fast 486 PC with 8 MB of RAM to use *Worlds Chat* effectively.

2 Click once more on the portrait and the image will become a rotating 3-D animation. To choose this avatar, click the *Accept* button. A larger view of your avatar now appears.

3 The *Guest User* box will be checked. Click the *Enter Worlds Chat* button to connect to the *Worlds Chat* server and enter the space station.

How to Communicate

As with conventional on-line chat systems, all communication in *Worlds Chat* is carried out via the keyboard, and anything you "say" appears on screen for all users to read unless you choose to "whisper" privately to a specific user (see tip box on the right).

Main Screen
In Worlds Chat *you can move around, interact with other avatars, and pass through doors to explore the space station. You view the station from a first-person perspective.*

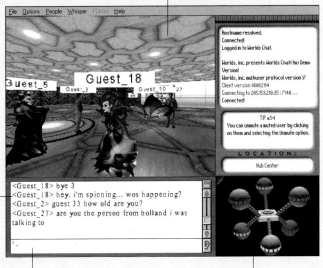

Speech Box
This box shows all speech and the names of the speakers. Whispered chat does not appear here.

Input Box
To chat with other users, type your words in this box. Then transmit them by pressing the Return key.

Map
Click any of the globes in this map panel to teleport to a different location in the space station.

Can I Speak Privately?
If you want to speak privately to a specific user without everyone "listening," click on that person's avatar and choose *Whisper to* from the drop-down menu. The avatar's name will appear in the speech box followed by a colon. Alternatively, just type the avatar's name, followed by a colon. This is known as "whispering."

Hub Center
You can return to the Hub Center (where you enter Worlds Chat*) by clicking the center of the map.*

EXPLORING THE ENVIRONMENT

Moving around in *Worlds Chat* is easy. You simply use the direction keys on your keyboard to move forward, backward, left, and right; use the mouse to make fine adjustments. Clicking on the screen suspends all movement, and a walking man icon appears. To resume movement, click on this icon.

ROOMS AND CORRIDORS

The space station contains many rooms devoted to different themes. These rooms are linked by corridors and escalators. You can also move to different levels by using the space station's elevators.

Air Walk Corridor

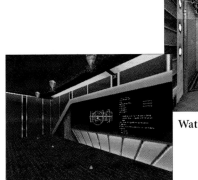

Water Lift

Engineering Control Center

Languages: Spanish and French

WorldsAway

WorldsAway, a virtual world developed by Fujitsu Cultural Technologies, is currently only available to *CompuServe* subscribers. *WorldsAway* uses avatars to represent people in a virtual environment centered on live chat. It also has its own forum in which you can discuss every aspect of this virtual world and download additional software, and a virtual economy (based on "tokens"). Each avatar is capable of a range of movements and facial expressions. Users can change their clothing, color, and even their heads and bodies, as often as they wish, providing they have "earned" enough tokens to afford it. The result is a program that blends keyboard-based chat with a highly visual means of expressing humor, emotion, and body language, and with something not far removed from on-line shopping.

THE DREAMSCAPE

The *WorldsAway* "dreamscape" is made up of a series of screens that your avatar navigates through. Because you don't see the world through the eyes of your avatar, you are constantly aware of how your avatar appears to others, and how it relates to the virtual space and the people in it.

COMMUNICATING

These examples show some of the main areas where people convene in Phantasus. This city (shown in the examples on these pages) contains many buildings and locations, mostly devoted to different themes or activities.

YOUR AVATAR
WorldsAway avatars can look as normal or strange as you wish. New users tend to look fairly normal. Those with green skins and broccoli for heads have probably been around a little longer!

Getting Up and Running
To run *WorldsAway*, you must be a *CompuServe* subscriber. You will also need the *WorldsAway* software (you can get this from *CompuServe*). To enter *WorldsAway*, connect to *CompuServe*, click the traffic light icon on the menu bar, type **away** in the *Go* box, and press the Return key.

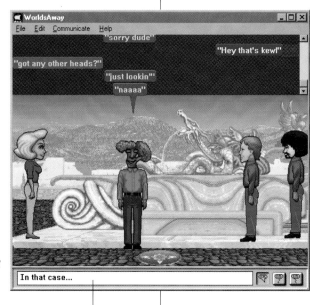

Ghosting
At any time you can choose to become a "ghost" and retain a degree of anonymity. Your presence is represented by a cloud icon, but your identity is secret. You can eavesdrop or "lurk" as you might in a newsgroup (see page 88).

Look Who's Talking
As with IRC, you can only talk openly with people on your "channel" (screen). For clarity, each avatar's words are displayed in a different color. Click on an avatar to read his or her name.

Speech Box

Moving Around
In this two-dimensional environment, movement is controlled by menus. To access a menu with a choice of movement options, click on the ground, an avatar, or an object.

Keyboard Chat
"Talk" by typing in the speech box and pressing Return. The three buttons (from left to right) let you "talk aloud," "think," or "ESP" respectively. Thoughts appear in a "thinks" bubble; ESP is for private messages. You can ESP someone on a different screen to you, as long as he or she is currently in the dreamscape.

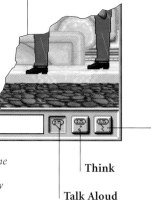

ESP

Think

Talk Aloud

MONEY EXCHANGE IN WORLDSAWAY

The virtual token-based economy of *WorldsAway* is the driving force behind much of the activity that goes on there. Before you enter the world, you are given some tokens to start you off, and many newbies immediately ask where to get more. You "earn" tokens by spending time in *WorldsAway* and by winning competitions (see box below). Every hour will earn you 60 tokens. You can even rent a "turf" (your own virtual apartment) for a monthly fee.

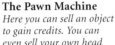

The Pawn Machine
Here you can sell an object to gain credits. You can even sell your own head to buy a new one at a head-vending machine.

Check Your Balance
You use an Automated Token Machine (ATM) to check your account or withdraw tokens.

Go Shopping
You can spend your tokens at one of the many "vendroid" vending machines.

Change How You Look
To change your avatar's appearance, you can buy a new head or body, or body paint, from various vending machines.

ADDING A PHYSICAL DIMENSION

In IRC, emoticons are used to evoke tone or mood within a text-based environment (see page 99). In *WorldsAway*, each avatar can display a range of gestures, actions, and facial expressions to convey emotion and humor. You can choose these from a drop-down menu or corresponding function keys.

Happy   **Normal**   **Sad**   **Angry**

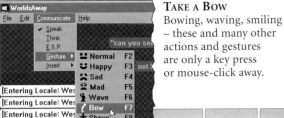

TAKE A BOW
Bowing, waving, smiling – these and many other actions and gestures are only a key press or mouse-click away.

Shrug   **Wave**   **Bow**

On-Line Gaming and Plug-Ins

Plug-in games are available for *WorldsAway*. You can use these to play on-line against other avatars. There are also many "official" activities and events, all advertised in the *Kymer Clarion*, one of the *WorldsAway* newsletters. Further details are available from the *Community Forum*.

Bingo
The avatar who is currently "host" will announce the rules for this version of Bingo *(written by Eddie Geoghegan), call the numbers, and award the prizes.*

Joining a Game
To join an on-going game of bingo, launch the Bingo *program, wait until the host announces a new game, then click the* Register *button and follow the host's instructions.*

The On-Line Services

The main difference between on-line service providers (OSPs) and other Internet service providers is that OSPs offer a wide range of customer-only content, such as on-line dictionaries, encyclopedias, news services, real-time stock market prices, and airline and train timetables. It is easy to communicate with other customers using e-mail or by chatting on-line. (See pages 26-7 for a brief comparison of OSPs and Internet service providers.) This section shows some of the areas common to the on-line services, and the software you need to access them. It also tells you how to sign up for a trial account.

Organized On-Line Environments

Most OSPs now offer Internet access, but their main feature is the privately maintained network that is only accessible to customers. This network is not part of the Internet, although some OSPs are currently making some content available on the Web. The customer-only networks share many of the Internet features described in this book – for example, e-mail, file transfer, search tools, and newsgroups. But the biggest advantage of the on-line services for many users is their organization. Because OSPs control the structure and content of their networks, they are more logical and user-friendly environments – especially for beginners. These pages show some of the shared features of the main OSPs: *America Online* (*AOL*), *CompuServe*, and *The Microsoft Network* (*MSN*).

INTERNATIONAL CONTENT

Since the main on-line services are available in many countries, some of the content they offer is country-specific. *MSN* subscribers, for example, can view this material by choosing *Worldwide Categories* from the *Categories* window.

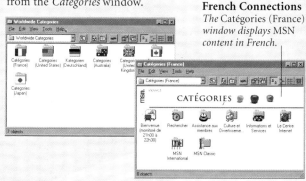

French Connections
The Catégories (France) *window displays* MSN *content in French.*

ON-LINE SHOPPING

All the on-line services provide shopping areas where you can view images and descriptions of a wide range of goods and services before deciding if you want to buy.

Viewing the Goods
The MSN Mall *window shows a typical example of an on-line shopping area. Here you can preview and order a wide range of products.*

GAMING

On-line gaming has always been a popular feature of the on-line services. *CompuServe's Fun and Games* area takes you to a wealth of shareware and on-line games, and gives you the opportunity to communicate with other games players.

On-Line Games
Kesmai's Air Warrior *is a popular multiplayer aerial combat game. Click* Air Warrior *on the* Games Site *page. From here you can download and launch the game.*

SUBJECT-SPECIFIC AREAS

Careful organization of content is one of the main features of the on-line services. In *CompuServe* you will find hundreds of forums that share the same structure. The Association of Shareware Professionals forum is a typical example. Here you can download files via the *Library* menu, read and post newsgroup-like messages via the *Messages* menu, chat with other visitors to the forum, or take part in live conferences.

Software and Support

Since many on-line forums are maintained by software companies and developers, they can be ideal places for asking questions related to product support.

MEMBER SERVICES

On-line help for customers is easily accessible in the on-line services. The "help" features in *AOL* are clearly signposted in the *Member Services* area. These include advice on account management and local access numbers.

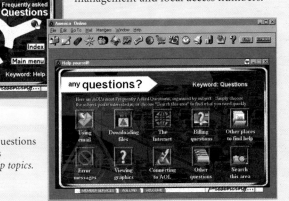

AOL FAQs

The Frequently Asked Questions *area of* Member Services *contains many useful help topics.*

INTERNET ACCESS

You can connect to the Internet using the software supplied by the OSP. From *AOL*'s *Internet* area, for example, you can access the Web (using *AOL*'s own browser) as well as browsing easily accessible help files.

FTP with AOL

You can download software and files to your hard disk using AOL's selection of FTP sites from around the world.

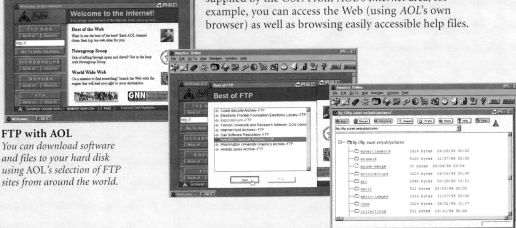

America Online

America Online (*AOL*) was launched in the US in the early 1990s and is now regarded as one of the leading on-line services. *AOL* has been available in a number of European countries since 1996.

AOL's Channels Window

AOL's main menu is available from the *Channels* window. You can create shortcuts to your favorite or most commonly visited sites by clicking the *Favorite Places* icon on the toolbar. This opens the *Favorite Places* window, where you can add, remove, or organize your shortcuts.

NAVIGATING THROUGH AOL
AOL's main menu covers a wide area of interests, including international news, home shopping, health and fitness, and children's interests.

Learning and Culture
The Learning and Culture *window is a typical* AOL *category window. It contains many links to areas devoted to education, reference works, and arts-related subjects. Clicking on* The Arts *link takes you to a further specialized screen.*

The Arts
On this screen, arts-related areas are provided in a list, and colorful buttons provide links to special areas of interest.

AOL TOOLBAR
The *AOL* toolbar is always displayed at the top of the main *AOL* window.

File Search
Lets you select from thousands of files to download.

Mailbox
Alerts you to incoming e-mail.

Channels
Gives access to AOL's content by category.

Today's News
Provides a 24-hour news service.

World Wide Web
Gives direct access to the Web.

What's Hot
Shows new and exciting areas to explore.

People Connection
Lets you chat "live" with other members.

Stocks and Porfolios
Gives up-to-date Wall Street information.

Date and Time
Provides an on-line clock.

Member Services
Provides free on-line support from AOL.

Favorite Places
User-definable menu of links.

Find
Lets you search for details about other AOL members.

Compose E-Mail
Lets you write and send e-mail messages.

Marketplace
Provides an on-line shopping facility.

My AOL
Allows you to customize your AOL settings.

Print
Prints current file or page.

Personal Filing Cabinet
Lets you view saved e-mails and downloaded files.

Keyword
Allows you to go directly to any AOL area using keywords.

CompuServe

CompuServe was founded in 1969 in the US and now offers more than 3,000 different services to over 4.5 million customers worldwide. Like *AOL* and *MSN*, it offers country-specific content. The example below shows the interface seen by customers in the UK, using *CompuServe*'s *WinCim* software for Windows.

International Features

CompuServe's main menu appears in the *Explore Services* window. You can explore the main content areas by clicking any of the sixteen category buttons. To save shortcuts to your favorite areas in *CompuServe*, click the *Favorite Places* button on the toolbar. In the *Favorite Places* window that appears, you can add, remove, or edit your shortcuts.

Some CompuServe Features

❑ On-line *Hutchinson Encyclopedia*

❑ *CB Simulator* – over 100 channels for live chat with people throughout the world

❑ *CNN Online* from Cable News Network and *PA News* from the Press Association

❑ *WorldsAway* "virtual world" (see pages 106-7)

❑ Home shopping via the *Electronic Shopping Mall*

❑ *KidsNet* – entertainment for children

COMPUSERVE NEWS WINDOW
From the *News* window, you can access current news from the Press Association's wide-ranging news service, and browse Web pages of some UK daily newspapers. You can also search all UK newspapers via the *UK Newspaper Library*. (This service attracts additional charges.)

Cable Network News Area
The CNN Interactive *area provides news, discussion forums, and access to the CNN Web page.*

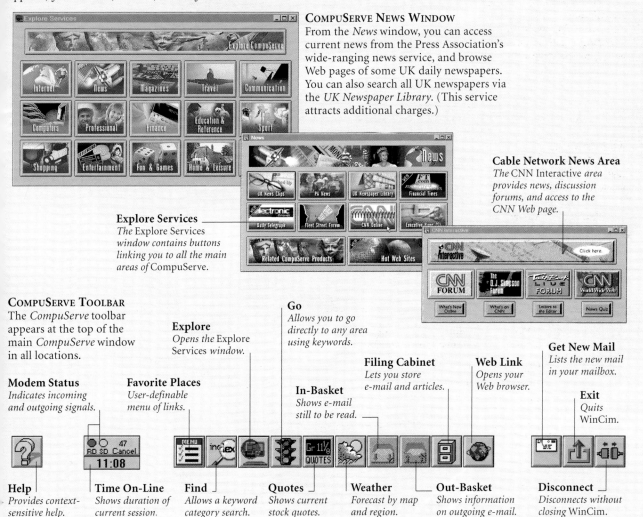

Explore Services
The Explore Services *window contains buttons linking you to all the main areas of* CompuServe.

COMPUSERVE TOOLBAR
The *CompuServe* toolbar appears at the top of the main *CompuServe* window in all locations.

Explore
Opens the Explore Services *window.*

Go
Allows you to go directly to any area using keywords.

Filing Cabinet
Lets you store e-mail and articles.

Web Link
Opens your Web browser.

Get New Mail
Lists the new mail in your mailbox.

Modem Status
Indicates incoming and outgoing signals.

Favorite Places
User-definable menu of links.

In-Basket
Shows e-mail still to be read.

Exit
Quits WinCim.

Help
Provides context-sensitive help.

Time On-Line
Shows duration of current session.

Find
Allows a keyword category search.

Quotes
Shows current stock quotes.

Weather
Forecast by map and region.

Out-Basket
Shows information on outgoing e-mail.

Disconnect
Disconnects without closing WinCim.

The Microsoft Network

The Microsoft Network (MSN) is the newest of the leading on-line services. It was released to coincide with the launch of Windows 95. The MSN software is included with Windows 95 and is designed to integrate closely with the operating system.

MSN Central

The Microsoft Network's main window, called MSN Central, contains five buttons. Click the Categories button to view the content categories for MSN. You can create a shortcut to any file or location by clicking its icon and clicking the Add to Favorites button on the MSN toolbar. These shortcuts are saved in the Favorite Places window.

MSN Central
The main MSN *screen has a useful link to the* Member Assistance *area. This contains help files, a member directory, and information on how* MSN *is organized.*

Information & Services
The Information & Services *window contains links to bulletin boards (*MSN *newsgroups), software libraries, documents, and windows containing further subcategories.*

TOOLBAR

The Microsoft Network's toolbar will be very familiar to Windows 95 users: it is essentially a modified version of the standard toolbar used for all windows.

Go to a Different Folder
Click this to access a drop-down menu of MSN *folders.*

Go to MSN Central

Properties
Shows the Properties of a file or location.

Sign Out
Disconnects from MSN.

Large Icons
Shows contents as large icons.

Small Icons
Shows contents as small icons.

Details
Shows contents as a detailed list.

Up One Level
Moves you to the folder containing the active folder.

Go to Favorite Places
Opens the Favorite Places *window.*

Add to Favorite Places
Adds a shortcut icon in the Favorite Places *window.*

List
Displays contents as a list.

Software for On-Line Services

E ach on-line service provider produces its own unique software; you use this to access both the on-line service and the Internet. Signing up with an OSP is a straightforward matter. You are usually offered a free limited-period trial account when you install the software. This software is free, and available from the sources listed below.

Where to Find the Software

❑ **Free CDs or disks**
Cover disks included with PC and Internet magazines.

❑ **Direct from on-line service providers**
Call them (they advertise their telephone numbers widely in the media) and ask for the a copy of their software.

❑ **From the Web (for AOL and CompuServe)**
Download the software for AOL and CompuServe from their Web sites (see box on this page).

❑ **From Windows 95 (for MSN)**
Software for MSN is included with Windows 95. You may need to install it from your Windows 95 CD or disks.

INSTALLING THE SOFTWARE
To install an on-line service's software and register for a trial account, simply follow any instructions on screen during installation, read the information files, and (if you intend to proceed) supply your name, address, and payment (credit card) details when prompted. It is usually possible to install the software and register for a free trial account within about 30 minutes.

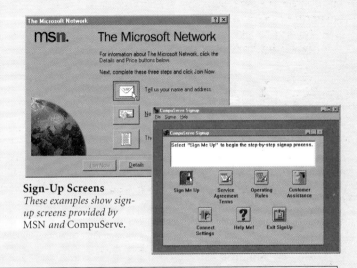

Sign-Up Screens
These examples show sign-up screens provided by MSN and CompuServe.

> ### Canceling Your Trial Account
> If you have signed up for a trial account with an on-line service provider, but do not intend to take out a full one, you can cancel your subscription on-line at any time from the "accounts" or "billing" areas before the trial period has expired. If you don't cancel, you may be charged for a full account.

Visit the Web Page

If you are interested in trying one of the on-line services described on these pages, it is strongly recommended that you first visit their Web sites for up-to-date information. The nature of the on-line services is changing rapidly. It was only in 1996 that Internet access became a standard feature of the main on-line services, and the trend for on-line service providers is toward a more Web-based presence. Software is regularly updated. Pricing plans are also regularly reviewed, and may vary from one country to another. You can access the main on-line services' Web sites at:
http://www.aol.com
http://www.compuserve.com
http://www.msn.com

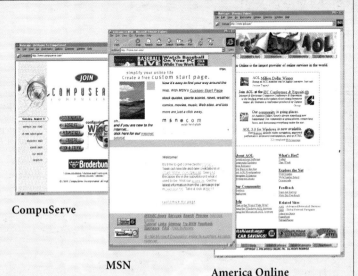

CompuServe

MSN

America Online

Troubleshooting

With so many separate elements making up an Internet transaction – not only your own PC, modem, and software, but your provider's server, the public telephone service, and the many bridges and gateways that connect the various world-wide networks – it is hardly surprising that things sometimes don't work as they should. These problems can usually be solved by taking a logical and systematic approach to fault-finding. The following pages illustrate some typical problems you might encounter, from connections not working, to the sometimes obscure error codes that are thrown up by the Web.

General Connection Problems

I CAN'T CONNECT TO MY SERVICE PROVIDER

❑ Make a thorough check of all your hardware connections, ensuring that your PC, modem, and telephone links are in place and correct.

❑ Ensure that your personal details – identification, node name and passwords – have been entered correctly in your dial-up software (see pages 36-9).

❑ Call your service provider and ask whether they are aware of connection problems at their end.

MY MODEM KEEPS GETTING AN ENGAGED SIGNAL

❑ It might be that demand is so high that the lines to your provider are all taken. If you keep trying you should eventually get connected.

❑ The software you use to dial in to your service provider may be configured with the wrong telephone number.

❑ The problem could also be caused if the modem is set up incorrectly – review the settings you typed when setting up your modem (see pages 23 and 24).

Other Connection Problems

If you have problems sending or receiving e-mails or accessing newsgroups:

❑ Check your e-mail and newsreader software have been configured correctly with the names for your service provider's news and mail servers (see page 33).

❑ Your service provider's mail server or news server may be temporarily "down" for repair or maintenance. Try to connect again later. If the problem persists, call your service provider's help line.

If you can't log on to an FTP site:

❑ Check that the address you have typed for the FTP server is accurate. If you still have difficulties, it may be that the server is temporarily out of action. It is also possible that you are not allowed access to that server. You will not be able to log on via anonymous FTP to a server that does not permit public access (see page 42).

MY CONNECTION IS TOO SLOW OR UNRELIABLE

❑ This is usually a result of modem speed. Nowadays a 14.4K modem is the recommended minimum for connecting to the Internet, but 28.8K modems will give better results.

❑ The problem could also relate to the speed of the server you are connecting to, or the amount of activity it is handling at that time. If connection speed improves the next time you log on, the problem may only have been temporary.

❑ Check that the initialization software on your modem has been set correctly – it may be that your modem has inadvertently been set up to perform at a slow speed. Once again, line noise can slow things down, so reconnecting might solve the problem.

Problems on the Web

One of the most frustrating experiences when using the World Wide Web is failing to connect to a page. When this happens (or, rather, fails to happen) click your Web browser's "Stop" button and try to make a new connection. Sometimes, however, the problem is a little more deep-rooted, and you will get a short, numbered error message. The most common error codes begin with the numbers four or five. Four usually means that the problem is at your end. Five usually indicates a server fault. Here are the most common error codes you are likely to encounter, and some advice on how to deal with them:

UNAUTHORIZED 401
This usually occurs if you need to enter identification and password to access a site. It may be that you have mis-typed your personal details or that you are not authorized to enter the site.

FORBIDDEN 403
When you visit certain Web servers, they check the domain name of your Internet service provider. This enables them to deny entry to certain users; for example, those seeking access from specific countries. This error code can also denote a server problem. It is becoming increasingly common as the number of secure or restricted sites increases.

NOT FOUND 404
This is the most common error message you are likely to encounter. It usually results from an incorrectly coded link or a bad address. Usually, the site you are trying to link to has been withdrawn, or possibly moved to a different server. A change-of-address hot link is usually shown on such pages for a limited period.

INTERNAL ERROR 500
The server containing the Web site encountered a problem and could not carry out your request. This may be a one-off problem, so try to connect again. If the error recurs, e-mail the Web page owner and explain the problem.

SERVICE TEMPORARILY OVERLOADED 502
The server cannot process your request because of the high load of requests currently being processed. Try again at a later time.

GATEWAY TIMEOUT 503
There is either a problem at a different server, or at one of the many possible network links that the information passes along before it arrives on your PC.

UNABLE TO LAUNCH VIEWER 16
If this error message appears when you try to download a file, it is usually because the browser does not have a "helper application" assigned to this file type. You may need to adjust your browser's settings to solve this problem. (See "How Browsers Handle File Types" on page 72.)

IS THE ADDRESS ACCURATE?
If you are having connection problems, always check first that you have typed the correct address. Most addresses are lower case, but some require an exact combination of upper and lower case letters.

Ask for Help...

❏ **From Your Service Provider**

If you can't fix a problem yourself, after following the advice on these pages, contact your Internet service provider. Most ISPs provide a telephone help line – you pay for the service, so don't be afraid to use it. If your problem is software-specific, contact the developer or supplier of your software. Many software developers offer telephone or on-line support via their Web pages.

❏ **On the Internet**

Use the extensive on-line help resources on the Internet. You can find many newsgroups devoted to Internet use and to specific software. Remember to read each newsgroup's FAQ document. You will probably find that someone has had the same problem as you and that a helpful user has posted a solution.

For more information about any of the activities described in this book, refer to Appendix 4. This provides a list of useful Web sites and Internet-related documents on everything from e-mail to Web browsers.

APPENDIX 2

Common File Formats

Many files on the Internet have been compressed or encoded in some way. Both types of files can contain a wide range of file formats, such as programs, text, images, and multimedia files. Compressing files can reduce their size considerably, saving you valuable download time. Encoding files makes them suitable for transmission over the Internet via e-mail and other services that were originally designed to carry text rather than binary data. Encoded files can contain compressed files. These pages describe the main types of compressed and encoded files you will need to recognize on the Internet, and advise you on how to handle them.

Compressed Files

You will regularly encounter compressed files on the Internet, especially on FTP sites. Compressed files are used for two main reasons. First, compressing a file can reduce it by up to 95 percent of its original size. This saves time when downloading the file. Secondly, a compressed file allows several files of different types to be stored in a single file. For example, a compressed file for a piece of shareware can contain a program, data files, a readme file, and various other related documents. It is clearly much easier to be able to download all these files in one operation. The box on the opposite page lists the main compressed file types for PC users and suggests how to expand them. It also refers to shareware programs for handling compressed files.

The example below shows how to expand a *.zip* file, using a program called *WinZip*. If this program is installed on your PC, follow the steps below.

Self-Extracting Compressed Files

Self-extracting compressed files usually have an *.exe* (program) extension. To run a self-extracting program, you simply double-click the file's icon. In some cases, a set-up routine will begin automatically, and you will be asked where you want to place the extracted files. (See "Installing Shockwave" on page 71.)

In other cases, the extracted files are placed loose in the folder that contains the *.exe* file. If this folder already contains lots of files, it can be difficult to identify exactly which files you have just extracted. It is therefore recommended that you create a new folder for every file with an *.exe* extension that you download. This enables you to store all the extracted files together in a single folder.

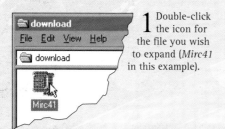

1 Double-click the icon for the file you wish to expand (*Mirc41* in this example).

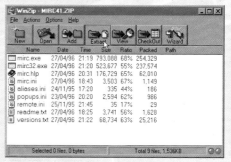

2 The *WinZip* window displays names of all the files contained in the *.zip* file. Click the *Extract* button.

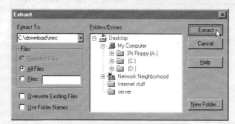

3 In the *Extract* dialog box, navigate to a folder in which to extract the files. You can type a new folder name in the *Extract To* box. Click *Extract*.

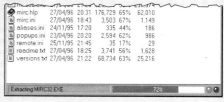

4 A progress bar at the bottom of the window indicates that the *.zip* file is being expanded. When the process is complete, the decompressed files will appear in the folder you specified in Step 3. You can now use these files.

Common Compressed File Formats

DOS/Windows-Based Files
The file extensions for the compressed file formats you will most commonly use are:

.zip .arj .lzh .arc

UNIX-Based Files
The following files relate to the UNIX operating system. (You may have difficulty using them after expansion, depending on the software you have on your PC.)

.z .gz .tar

The UNIX operating system's TAR program will combine several files (similar to a .zip file). These may include .z and gz files. Such files will have the extensions .tar.z or .tar.gz (also called .tgz).

Self-Extracting Archives
Some files with the .exe extension may be self-extracting compressed files (see box on opposite page).

Useful Expansion Programs
You will find many good programs to view and extract compressed files. Two good examples are WinZip (available as shareware from **http://www.winzip.com***) and Stuffit Expander (available as freeware from many sites, including* **http://www.windows95.com***). The latest versions of these programs are fully compatible with Windows 95, and can handle all the compressed file formats referred to on this page. You can use Winzip to make your own compressed files – a good idea if you want to free up hard disk space. Stuffit Expander will also decode certain types of encoded files, such as the .uu and .uue formats (see "Encoded Files" below).*

Encoded Files

You are most likely to download encoded files as part of an e-mail message – when someone has sent you an attachment as part of a message – or as a binary file from a newsgroup (see page 93). Encoding turns binary data into plain text, enabling it to be sent as e-mail. Your mail program or newsreader should have the capability to decode the attached text, image, or program file for you, but occasionally it may not recognize the encoding format. In this case, you need to use a program such as *Wincode* (available as freeware from **http://www.global2000.net/users/snappy/snappy/wincode.html**).

The example here shows how to use *Wincode* to decode an encoded file that you have downloaded to your hard disk. First launch *Wincode*, then follow these steps.

1 Click the *Decode a data file* button.

2 In the *File to Decode* box, navigate to the folder on your hard disk that contains the encoded file, highlight it, and click *OK*.

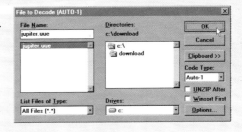

Other File Formats

Even if your decompression or decoding software can handle a file type, this does not necessarily mean that you can use it on your PC. For example, files with the extensions *.bin, .hqx, .sit, .sea,* and *.image* are Apple Macintosh files. Their contents may be viewable on your PC, depending on the original format (for example, you may be able to read text files), but usability is not guaranteed. As a general rule, it is sensible to avoid these file types.

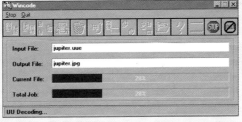

3 The *Wincode* window displays the name of the encoded file, and the decoded file it is creating. The *Wincode Done!* box pops up when decoding is complete.

4 Click *OK* in the *Wincode Done!* box. You can now open the file (in this case, a *.jpg* image file) using a suitable program.

Useful Web Pages

The Web sites in this Appendix will provide you with further information on most of the Internet activities described in this book. Most of these sites contain many links to other similar sites. The "software" section will point you to sites that offer hundreds of thousands of freeware and shareware programs. This concise Web directory is divided into the following sections:

- Primers/Reference • FTP • Software • E-mail • Gopher • Telnet • Newsgroups
- Gaming Resources • VRML • "Live" Chat • On-line services

The best jumping-off points for exploring the Web are the many Web-based search engines (described on page 76). As well as excellent search capabilities, many of these sites provide large Web directories organized by subject (often with descriptions and ratings for each site), and some contain "What's New" or "What's Cool" sites.

Primers/Reference

Beginners Central
http://www.digital-café.com/ ~webmaster/begin00.html
Beginners' guide to all aspects of the Internet. Provides background information on e-mail, newsgroups, the Web, and other common Internet activities.

Newbie NET
http://www.newbie.net
This site offers a "Cyber Course" that introduces beginners to a host of Internet activities, such as e-mail, Web browsing, downloading files with FTP, and using MUDs and talkers.

Internet Tool References
http://www.ug.cs.dal.ca/pub/ online-dir/internet/Index.html
Provides links to sites containing information on FTP, e-mail, networks, Telnet, Usenet, and other general Internet guides.

Internet Resources
http://www.brandonu.ca/~ennsnr/ Resources/Welcome.html
Links to many useful Internet guides and resource lists, as well as FTP archives and FAQs. Also contains links to newsgroups and mailing lists devoted to Internet-related discussion.

Beginner's Luck
http://www.execpc.com/%7Ewmhogg/ beginner.html
A comprehensive list of Internet resources, including search engines, guides and tutorials, lists of graphics and multimedia files and the programs you need to view them, and links to virtual libraries on the Web.

Internet Help and Training Resources
http://www.ub2.lu.se/NNC/guide/ inethelp.html
Provides information on all aspects of the Internet, such as URLs, e-mail, file formats, training resources, and HTML. Includes a glossary of common Internet terms.

Learn the Net
http://www.learnthenet.com
Covers all the basic information new Internet users need to know - everything from how an e-mail address works to how to exchange files over the Net. This site can be viewed in a number of languages.

EFF's (Extended) Guide to the Internet
http://www.cosy.sbg.ac.at/doc/eegtti
Beginners' Internet guide produced by the Electronic Frontier Foundation. Has useful information on public-access Internet providers and on-line services around the world.

Hypertext Database of Thousands of Internet FAQs
http://www.cis.ohio-state.edu/ hypertext/faq/usenet/FAQ-List.html
This large list of Internet FAQs is arranged alphabetically. A search tool is also provided at this site.

Internet Information Center
http://www.iic.priv.at/iic
Contains an introduction to the Internet that covers its history and explains some technical features, such as IP addressing. Also contains useful "how to" sections on the main Internet activities, and an Internet glossary.

Internet and Web Help
http://www.earthlink.net/netfaqs/ main.html
Provides a list of sites that cover all aspects of the Internet. Also has Windows 95-specific FAQs and help sections on Windows Internet software.

InterNic Documentation
http://ds.internic.net/ds/ dspg0intdoc.html
Database dedicated to discussion on the future development of the Internet, and the work of the Internet Engineering Task Force (IETF).

Internet Starter Kit
http://www.mcp.com/hayden/iskm/windows.html
Complete on-line version of the guide for Windows users by Hayden Books. Contains sections on the Internet and its history, and on how to connect to the Internet.

Net Resources
http://www.eit.com/goodies/resources
Includes the Internet Resources list. This contains links to hundreds of Internet information services and resources.

Yanoff's Internet Services List
http://www.spectracom.com/islist
Huge list of Internet links, arranged by category. Includes "What's New" and "What's Cool" sections.

Netiquette Home Page
http://www.rs6000.adm.fau.edu/rinaldi/netiquette.html
How to behave on the Internet; covers all the main activities on the Net.

Microsoft Support Online
http://www.microsoft.com/support
From this site you can access the Microsoft Knowledge Base, FAQs on Microsoft's Internet products, and Microsoft newsgroups.

Cutter's Windows 95 Crossroads
http://www.io.com/~kgk/win95.html
Links to Web sites, and newsgroups devoted to Microsoft-related issues.

FTP

File Transfer Protocol FAQs
http://www.net-link.net/faq/ftpfaq.html
Contains links to several useful FTP sites and FAQs. Also provides information about anonymous FTP and using the FTP features of Netscape Navigator.

Monster FTP Sites List
http://hoohoo.ncsa.uiuc.edu/ftp
Huge list of FTP sites arranged alphabetically by server name.

Tile.net
http://tile.net/ftp-list/
Guide to anonymous FTP sites, arranged by contents, country, domain, and site name.

Archie Request Form
http://hoohoo.ncsa.uiuc.edu/archie.html
Use this page to submit an Archie search of FTP sites via the Web.

FTP Search
http://ftpsearch.ntnu.no/ftpsearch
Powerful search tool for FTP sites. Includes on-line help.

Software

Windows95.com
http://www.windows95.com
Contains a large shareware library, tutorials, and information specifically for Windows 95 users. Also contains an Internet "Hyper-Glossary."

Shareware.com
http://www.shareware.com
Cnet's site provides a wealth of shareware you can download, and has a searchable index of shareware sites on the Internet.

Software Library
http://home.zdnet.com
Provides access to a large shareware library, with over 10,000 files that you can download, and Web pages for Ziff-Davis magazines in the US and Europe.

TUCOWS (The Ultimate Collection of Winsock Software)
http://www.tucows.com
A collection of shareware and freeware, particularly for Windows users. Includes a search facility. This page offers you a list of mirror sites in many regions and countries. Choose the nearest one to you for speedier downloads.

Jumbo Shareware
http://www.jumbo.com
Searchable collection of over 70,000 freeware and shareware programs, organized by category. Also has starter kits for new users that include antivirus and decompression software.

Stroud's Consummate Winsock Applications
http://www.cwsapps.com
Searchable collection of many Internet programs and files. Also contains reviews of the latest Windows 95-compatible software.

E-Mail

FAQ: How to Find People's E-Mail Addresses
http://www.qucis.queensu.ca/FAQs/email/finding.html
Information on techniques to use when searching for someone's e-mail address.

Perspectives on E-Mail
http://www.valley.net/~vue/email.html
Information and tutorials on e-mail, troubleshooting, mailing lists, and listservs. You can also download e-mail programs from this site.

Publicly Accessible Mailing Lists
http://www.NeoSoft.com/internet/paml/bysubj.html
Provides an alphabetical list of subject categories for mailing lists. You can also search for a mailing list by name.

A Beginner's Guide to Effective E-Mail
http://www.webfoot.com/advice/email.top.html
Recommendations on how to use e-mail effectively. This site also provides a dictionary of jargon terms and acronyms commonly used in messages on the Net.

World Wide Web

World Wide Web FAQs
http://www.boutell.com/faq
Answers to many frequently asked questions about the Web. Contains a wide range of information on the Web, its history, how it works, and to use it.

The World Wide Web Explained
http://www.smeal.psu.edu/~rob/web.html
Brief tutorial on the Web, with many links to sites or files that illustrate, for example, HTML, information resources, and multimedia on the Web.

World Wide Web Consortium
http://www.w3.org/pub/WWW
News, background, discussions, and information concerning every aspect of the Web. This site also hosts the WWW Virtual Library and the World Wide Web Journal.

Browser Watch
http://browserwatch.iworld.com
Provides up-to-date news on Web browsers, plug-ins, and ActiveX controls. You can download plug-ins from the "Plug-In Plaza" page, and ActiveX controls from the "ActiveX Arena" page.

WWW Viewer Test Page
http://www-dsed.llnl.gov/documents/WWWtest.html
Use "test" buttons on this page to test if your Web browser is capable of handling, for example, image, audio, and video files. If you do not have an appropriate viewer installed, you can download one from this site.

Web Page Design
http://www-3.one.net/explore/webpagedesign.html
Guidance for beginners on designing and creating Web pages. Provides links to pages on HTML, graphics, and design.

A Beginner's Guide to HTML
http://www.ncsa.uiuc.edu/General/Internet/WWW/HTMLPrimer.html
Beginner's guide to HTML from the National Center for Supercomputing Applications(NCSA). Provides links to other HTML-related resources on the Web.

Web/HTML Resource Page
http://www.webhaven.com/chen/webhtml
Provides HTML reference material suitable both for beginners and experts. Contains a primer, reference manuals, HTML standards, and HTML sample sites.

Microsoft Software
http://www.microsoft.com/download
You can download Microsoft's Internet Explorer from here, as well as many free Internet add-ons for Microsoft products.

Netscape Software
http://home.netscape.com
Netscape products, including the Navigator browser and plug-ins, can be downloaded via Netscape's home page.

Gopher

Gopher Jewels
http://galaxy.einet.net/GJ
Lists many of the best Gopher sites by category: from "Agriculture and Forestry" to "Travel Information." Each category contains links to many Gopher holes. A search tool is also provided.

Gophers Worldwide
gopher://gopher.tc.umn.edu:70/11/Other%20Gopher%20and%20Information%20Servers
List of worldwide gopher servers categorized by continent. Includes a search engine.

Veronica FAQ
gopher://gopher.scs.unr.edu:70/00/veronica/veronica-faq
Frequently asked questions about Veronica – the search and retrieval system for use with the Internet Gopher.

How to Compose Veronica Queries
gopher://gopher.scs.unr.edu:70/00/veronica/how-to-query-veronica
Basic and advanced techniques for submitting a Veronica query.

Telnet

Telnet (from "Zen and the Art of the Internet")
http://www.cs.indiana.edu/docproject/zen/zen-1.0_7.html
Description of Telnet and how to use it. This is Chapter 7 from "Zen and the Art of the Internet" – an on-line reference manual that contains useful material on many other Internet activities.

Telnet
http://hws3.hws.edu/www/Telnet.html
Description of how Telnet works. Includes a link to the Telnet site at the US Library of Congress.

Telnet Tips
http://galaxy.einet.net/hytelnet/TELNET.html
General guidelines to follow when logging on to and browsing Telnet sites.

Newsgroups

Usenet Information Center Launch Pad
http://sunsite.unc.edu/usenet-i
Information about Usenet newsgroups. From here you can browse selected groups via the Web and run a search for Usenet FAQs by name, subject, or keyword.

What is USENET?
http://www.sans.vuw.ac.nz/sans/ usenet.html
An introduction to Usenet newsgroups. The files here are a collection of FAQs found in the newsgroup news.announce.newusers.

Usenet FAQs
http://www.cis.ohio-state.edu/ hypertext/faq/usenet/top.html
Hypertext database containing thousands of Usenet FAQs found in the newsgroup news.answers. You can search or choose from an alphabetical list.

Usenet News
http://www.labcoll.nf.ca/~rick/training/ usenet/usenet.html
Contains a definition of Usenet news, a primer, and a FAQ. Also contains information on rules, etiquette, and style.

Gaming Resources

The Games Domain
http://www.gamesdomain.com
Extensive links to games, news about all aspects of on-line gaming, and cheats and hints for many popular computer games.

Interactive Games
http://www.nova.edu/ Inter-Links/interactive.html
The Nova Fun and Games site provides links to interactive games sites on the Internet, including a section on MUDs.

BU's Interactive WWW Games
http://www.bu.edu/Games/games.html
Links to many Web-based games (Java and non-Java).

Online Fun and Games Overdose
http://www.infocom.net/~romanm/ gamefun.html
Provides links to many Web sites dedicated to games (including leading games developers such as Sierra Online and Sega Online).

Fun'n'Games
http://208.5.14.241/funngames/
Links to on-line games, free games, and game reviews are available here. There is also a free area where you can buy, sell, and trade computer games.

VRML

VRMLSite Magazine
http://www.aereal.com/boom
A magazine that invites users to rate VRML sites. It also presents a VRML world chosen at random from somewhere on the Web and asks you to give it a "star" rating.

VRML Site of the Week
http://www.virtus.com/vrmlsite.html
This page features a VRML "site of the week." It shows an illustration, an artist's description, and a review for this and several other commended sites.

Virtual Reality Modeling Language
http://www.3dsite.com/cgi/ VRML-index.html
Large collection of links relating to VRML, including FAQs, tutorials, reference material, specifications, and VRML sites on the Web.

Superscape
http://www.superscape.com
Superscape's home page provides a direct link to their SuperCityII - a virtual city that you can explore. Other VRML worlds and models can be viewed using the Viscape browser plug-in.

"Live" Chat

Internet Relay Chat Information!
http://www2.undernet.org/~cs93jtl/ IRC.html
Comprehensive introduction to IRC, containing an introduction for beginners, technical information for more advanced users, and many links to documents, resources, and IRC-related newsgroups on the Internet.

The Benso.Com/IRC Help.Org Home Page
http://www.irchelp.org/
Another large and comprehensive IRC help site, containing links to IRC FAQs, primers, documents, help files, server lists, and maps. You can also download the mIRC client program from this site.

IRC FAQ
http://www.kei.com/irc.html
Concise IRC FAQ containing links to download sites for IRC client programs, and advice on which IRC servers to connect to.

WebChat Broadcasting Service
http://wbs.net
A Web-based chat site with many categories of "rooms" devoted to a wide range of themes and topics such as "Buddhist Chat," "Current Events Arena," and "Balloon Decorating and Twisting."

Chatting on the Net
http://www.yahoo.com/ Computers_and_Internet/Internet/ Chatting
Yahoo!'s regularly updated list of links to IRC sites, MUDs, MUSHes, Talkers, Web-based chat sites, and anything related to live on-line communication.

On-Line Services

America Online
http://www.aol.com
Information about America Online, up-to-date press releases, and links to new and useful site on the Web.

CompuServe
http://www.compuserve.com
Directories of selected sites on the Web, and the latest news about CompuServe.

The Microsoft Network
http://www.msn.com
Links to new sites on the Web, MSNBC news services, Internet FAQs, and Microsoft's software page.

Glossary

This glossary contains definitions for a number of technical terms used in this book and also for a selection of other Internet terms. Terms that are underlined refer to other glossary entries.

A,B

ACTIVEX
(see *JAVA*)

ANALOG DATA
The representation of information such as text, sound, and images as an electrical signal that varies in frequency and amplitude. Analog data can be transmitted over a standard telephone line. (See *binary data*.)

ANONYMOUS FTP
A method of logging on to a remote computer, using an *FTP* program, to *download* publicly accessible files held on that site.

APPLET
A small application that is *download*ed on demand and run via a *client program*.

ARCHIE
A regularly updated database of publicly accessible files and programs stored on *FTP* sites. Archie can be searched using a *client program*, *Web browser*, or by *e-mail*.

ASCII (AMERICAN STANDARD CODE FOR INFORMATION INTERCHANGE)
The international standard for converting text, digits, and punctuation into *binary data* that can be read by any computer. An ASCII text file is commonly called "plain text."

ATTACHMENT
A file that is linked to and sent with an *e-mail* message. Attachments can contain any type of file: a spreadsheet, graphics, sound, or program.

BACKBONE
The *Internet* backbone is a *network* of *supercomputer*s that are linked to each other through high-capacity lines that transfer data very quickly. The *Internet* backbone connects regional *network*s to each other and spans hundreds of thousands of miles.

BAUD RATE
A near obsolete measurement of transmission speed over a telephone line, sometimes confused with *bps*.

BBS (BULLETIN BOARD SYSTEM)
A single computer, or *network*, that you can dial direct to access discussion groups, games, software, and *e-mail* services. Since BBSs are not part of the *Internet*, a *direct internet connection* is not necessary to access them.

BETA VERSION
A version of a program that is still in the development stage and has not been released commercially. Beta programs are often distributed free over the *Internet* as part of the testing process. They inevitably contain bugs. Developers rely on users of the beta program to inform them of any problems.

BINARY DATA
Binary data consists of a series of 1s and 0s (bits), and is represented in a computer by the presence or absence of an electrical signal. *Analog data* must be converted into binary data before a computer can read it.

BINARY FILE
A file that contains nontextual data that cannot be stored as an *ASCII* file. A binary file can contain graphics, sound, or even programs.

BOOKMARK
A shortcut to an *Internet* site. Bookmarks can be stored and accessed via *Web browsers* and other *Internet* programs.

BPS (BITS PER SECOND)
A speed rating for computer *modem*s that measures the maximum number of bits per second that can be transferred over a standard telephone line under ideal conditions. A bit is the most basic unit of data.

BRIDGE
A device that connects separate local *network*s and allows data to be transferred between them.

BROWSER
(See *Web browser*)

C,D

CACHE DIRECTORY
An area of a computer's hard disk (usually a folder) in which the text and graphics of *Web page*s opened by a *Web browser* are stored. When you revisit a *Web page*, the *Web browser* looks in the cache to see if it can retrieve the data for that page instead of having to *download* it again.

CHANNEL
An area on an *IRC network* that people must join before they can *chat*. Some channels are devoted to specific subjects.

CHAT
A conversation on the *Internet*, between two or more people, in real time. Users type their part of the conversation at the keyboard. (See *IRC*.)

CLIENT PROGRAM
Software that requests services from, and exchanges data with, a *server*. Each client program is designed to work with specific types of *servers*. CuteFTP, for example, is a client program that connects to *FTP servers*.

CLIENT/SERVER
A concept used in *network* computing whereby computers are divided into two categories: *client*s and *servers*. A *client* requests information from a *server*. A *server* stores information and delivers it to any authorized *client* that requests it.

COM PORT
A computer operating system's name for a *serial port*.

COOKIE
A short string of text, containing information relating to your activity at a particular *Web site*, that is *download*ed to your hard disk and accessed the next time you visit that site. The information may contain details about goods you have ordered, for example.

DATA COMPRESSION
A way of reducing the size of a computer file by using special algorithms to make the file smaller and faster to transmit. You will need to expand a compressed file before you can use it.

DIAL-UP NETWORKING SOFTWARE
Windows 95 software that enables you to connect to your service *provider* and the *Internet*.

DIAL-UP SCRIPTING SOFTWARE
Windows 95 software that enables you to automate your *dial-up networking* connection to the *Internet*.

DIRECT INTERNET CONNECTION
A means of connecting directly to the *Internet* so that your computer becomes part of the *Internet* when you dial in (usually by *modem*). The two main *protocol*s that govern direct *Internet* connection by *modem* are *SLIP* and *PPP*.

DNS (DOMAIN NAME SYSTEM)
A database of domain names and their corresponding *IP address*es. When you type the name of an *Internet* site you wish to visit, a DNS *server* converts the name into its *IP address* so that the site can be located.

DOMAIN NAME
A domain name identifies a computer or subnetwork of computers on the *Internet*. All domain names end with an organization type or a two-letter country code. A domain name is a textual representation of a domain's *IP address*, and saves *Internet* users from having to memorize strings of numbers.

DOWNLOAD
The process of transferring a file from a remote computer to your computer.

DYNAMIC IP ADDRESSING
The process by which *Internet Service Provider*s assign temporary *IP address*es to their customers each time they connect to the *Internet*. These addresses are only valid for the duration of the connection. (See *Static IP Addressing*.)

E,F

E-MAIL (ELECTRONIC MAIL)
A system for sending messages between computers that are linked electronically over a *network*.

E-MAIL ADDRESS
An identifier that allows *e-mail* to be delivered to the correct computer or user.

EMOTICONS
Punctuation symbols used in *IRC*, *e-mail*, and *newsgroup* messages to convey emotions. Emoticons reveal a face when viewed sideways. A common emoticon is the smiley :-).

ENCRYPTION
The process of converting text into a special code so that it cannot easily be read by anyone other than the intended recipient. The recipient's software deciphers it using a special "key."

ERROR CORRECTION
A system of ensuring that noise on telephone lines has not introduced errors during data transmission. Error correction is performed by certain types of *modem*s.

FAQ (FREQUENTLY ASKED QUESTIONS)
A document containing common questions and answers on a particular subject. Many *Internet* FAQs are intended for *newbie*s. Most *newsgroup*s, and many other *Internet* sites, contain FAQS.

FAX-MODEM
A *modem* that can also act as a facsimile machine, enabling you to use your computer to send and receive faxes.

FREEWARE
Software that is distributed on the *Internet* for free use and redistribution, but the author retains copyright.

FTP (FILE TRANSFER PROTOCOL)
A *protocol* for transferring files on the *Internet* between all types of computers. Information is usually *download*ed from an *FTP server* using an *FTP client program* or a *Web browser*.

G,H

GATEWAY
A device that links *network*s together and can translate data between different types of *network*s.

GOPHER
A menu-based system that enables you to browse and retrieve files from Gopher *server*s.

GOPHERSPACE
The collective name for all the *Gopher server*s in the world.

HELPER APPLICATION
An application that enables programs such as *Web browser*s to handle *multimedia* files. A *browser* will usually launch a helper automatically whenever it is required.

HOME PAGE
The introductory page on a *Web site*. It usually contains a table of contents for the site and provides *hot links* to other pages.

HOT LINK
A shortcut that links to other *Web page*s or *Internet* sites.

HTML (HYPER TEXT MARKUP LANGUAGE)
The formatting language used to create *Web page*s. HTML is used for specifying how a page should look on screen. It can also embed *hypertext* links, images, sounds, and *applet*s into a page.

HTTP (HYPERTEXT TRANSPORT PROTOCOL)
The *protocol* used to retrieve documents that are pointed to by *hypertext* links on *Web page*s. These documents could be located anywhere on the *Internet*.

HYPERTERMINAL
A *modem* communications program supplied with Windows 95.

HYPERTEXT
Text that contains links to other parts of a document, or to documents held on another computer. Clicking a hypertext link takes you directly to the linked document. Hypertext links on *Web page*s are usually highlighted or underlined.

I,J,K

INTERNET
The linkage of a large number of computers around the world — ranging from personal computers to *supercomputers* — into one huge computer *network*. Every computer on the Internet uses the *TCP/IP protocol* to communicate, providing a vast database of information for anyone that can connect to it.

INTERNET SERVICE PROVIDER (ISP)
A commercial company that provides access to the *Internet* for a fee. Many ISPs also offer their own *Web page*s, *newsgroup*s, and *FTP* sites for their customers to use.

IP (INTERNET PROTOCOL)
A *protocol* that governs the way computers on the *Internet* communicate and exchange data with each other.

IP ADDRESS
A unique set of numbers assigned to every site on the *Internet* for the purpose of routing information to that site. An *IP* address corresponds to a site's *domain name*. An *IP* address may change - for example, if a site moves to another area of the *Internet. domain names* can stay the same: the *DNS server* will reconcile them with IP addresses.

IRC (INTERNET RELAY CHAT)
A series of *networks* on the *Internet* on which you can hold "live" conversations with people across the world. You access IRC with a *client program*, and use your keyboard to type in your part of the conversation.

ISDN (INTEGRATED SERVICES DIGITAL NETWORK)
A high-speed communications standard that enables a telephone line to carry voice and digital data at speeds higher than can be achieved with a *modem*.

JAVA
A programming language that is used, among other things, to embed small programs in *Web pages*. When you open a page your computer automatically runs the embedded program. JAVA *applet*s can appear as animations, or interactive elements such as spreadsheets or games, in the *Web browser* window or in a separate window. Microsoft's proprietary ActiveX system works in a similar way to JAVA.

L,M

LISTSERVER
An automated *e-mail* system used for sending the same message to many addresses simultaneously.

MAIL SERVER
A *server* that distributes outgoing *e-mail* messages, and stores incoming messages until users next connect to the *Internet* to collect them.

MAILING LIST
A list of *subscriber*s to an *e-mail*-based discussion group. When a *subscriber* sends an *e-mail* message to the mailing list's *listserver*, the *listserver* sends a copy of the message to every person on the list.

MIME (MULTIPURPOSE INTERNET MAIL EXTENSIONS)
A *protocol* that allows *binary files* to be sent via *e-mail*. MIME can be used with most types of computers.

MODEM (MODULATOR, DEMODULATOR)
An electronic device that allows remote computers to communicate with each other via a telephone line.

MUD (MULTIUSER DUNGEON)
A game - usually a text-based adventure or role-playing game - played simultaneously by many people over the *Internet*.

MULTIMEDIA
The inclusion of two or more media - text, graphics, audio, video, or animation, in a single program.

N,O

NETIQUETTE
An unwritten code of conduct for the proper and polite usage of the *Internet* - especially *newsgroups*.

NETWORK
A group of interconnected computers that can exchange information.

NEWBIE
A user who is new to the *Internet*.

NEWSGROUPS
Internet discussion groups, devoted to specific topics, in which people can *post* comments or information. The *network* of newsgroups is known as *Usenet*.

NEWSREADER
Software that allows you to *post* articles to *newsgroups*, and to read the articles other users have *post*ed.

NEWS SERVER
A *server* that distributes articles that are *post*ed to *newsgroups*. Messages eventually expire, and are removed from the *server*.

NODE
Any computer connected to a *network*.

OFF-LINE
Not currently connected to the *Internet* or a remote system.

ON-LINE
Currently connected to the *Internet* or a remote system.

ON-LINE SERVICE
A unique customer-only *network* of services provided by an *On-line Service Provider*. In many ways, these *network*s may be seen as a miniature version of the *Internet*, offering *newsgroups*, shopping, support services, and so on.

ON-LINE SERVICE PROVIDER
A company, such as CompuServe, that offers its customers *on-line service*s.

P,Q,R

PACKET SWITCHING
The method used to move data around the *Internet*. Data is broken into small "packets," each containing its source and destination address. The packets travel – sometimes via different routes – to their destination, where they are reassembled.

PLUG-IN
A program that adds features to a program such as a *Web browser*, so that it can handle file types containing, for example, 3-D and *multimedia* elements.

POP (POINT OF PRESENCE)
The telephone access number that customers use to dial in to their *Internet service provider*, and thus to the *Internet*. *Internet service provider*s often operate several regional POPs so that their customers can connect to the *Internet* via local phone services.

POP3 (POST OFFICE PROTOCOL)
A set of rules governing *servers* that store *e-mail* until it is collected by a user. With POP3 people can use any computer, not just their own, to connect to their mail server to collect their *e-mail* messages, by using a password.

POST
Articles sent to a *newsgroup* are said to be *post*ed, as they address a group rather than an individual.

PPP (POINT TO POINT PROTOCOL)
The most reliable and commonly used *protocol* that allows *direct internet connection*. It uses *TCP/IP* to connect computers to the *Internet* via a *modem*.

PROTOCOL
A set of rules that two computers must follow when they communicate. Software on *network*ed computers must be designed to implement these rules.

PROVIDER
See *Internet Service Provider* and *On-line Service Provider*.

ROUTER
A device used to move data around the *Internet*. Routers are part of the *packet switching* process: they read the address on a data packet and decide the best way to get it to its destination.

S,T

SEARCH ENGINE
Software that searches for specific information or files on the *Internet*, based on the criteria you give it. (Sometimes referred to as a search tool.)

SERIAL PORT
A port, or socket, on a computer for connecting an external device, such as a *modem* or a mouse.

SERVER
Any computer that allows you to connect to it and use or share its information and resources using a *client program*. The term also refers to the software that makes the information available for *download*ing.

SHAREWARE
Software that is made available for people to *download* and use for free, for a limited period. At the end of this trial period, you usually have to pay a fee if you want to continue using the software.

SLIP (SERIAL LINE INTERNET PROTOCOL)
A *protocol* that allows a *direct internet connection*, generally regarded as less reliable than a *PPP* connection. A *SLIP* connection uses *TCP/IP* to connect computers to the *Internet* via a *modem*.

SMTP (SIMPLE MAIL TRANSFER PROTOCOL)
A *protocol* used to transfer *e-mail* messages between computers.

STATIC IP ADDRESSING
The process by which *Internet Service Provider*s allocate a permanent *IP address* to each of their customers. (See *Dynamic IP Addressing*.)

STREAMING
Streaming is a way of playing sound and video files as they are *download*ing from a remote computer, rather than having to wait until the complete file has been copied to your hard disk. Many *Web browser plug-in*s support streaming.

SUBSCRIBE
The process of identifying the *newsgroups* you want to read each time you use your *newsreader*. Some *newsreader*s can automatically *download* new messages for the *newsgroups* you have subscribed to each time you log on.

SUPERCOMPUTER
An extremely fast and expensive computer usually used for scientific research. Supercomputers form a major part of the *Internet backbone*.

TALKER
A program that runs on a remote computer and allows two or more people to talk to each other in real time. You access a talker by using a *Telnet client program*.

TCP/IP (TRANSMISSION CONTROL PROTOCOL/INTERNET PROTOCOL)
The two core *Internet protocol*s that define how data must be transferred between computers. To have a *direct internet connection*, your computer must have TCP/IP software.

TELNET
A *protocol* that lets you log on to a remote computer and use it as if you were at that terminal.

U, V, W, X, Y, Z

UART CHIP (UNIVERSAL ASYNCHRONOUS RECEIVER/ TRANSMITTER)
This chip controls the flow of data through a computer's *serial port*. Fast *modem*s require fast UART chips, or their performance will be impaired.

URL (UNIFORM RESOURCE LOCATER)
An *Internet* address. URLs provide a standard syntax for referring to various Internet resources, including Web sites, *FTP* sites, *Gopher* sites, and so on.

USENET
The main *network* of *newsgroups* available via the *Internet*. Usenet access is also possible without a *direct internet connection*.

UUENCODE
A popular program for encoding *binary files* so that they can be transmitted by *e-mail*.

V STANDARDS
Worldwide telecommunications standards that govern factors such as programming commands and *data compression* standards used by *modem*s and other devices.

VERONICA (VERY EASY RODENT-ORIENTED NETWIDE INDEX TO COMPUTERIZED ARCHIVES)
A regularly-updated database of all the files in *Gopherspace* that you can query using keywords.

VRML (VIRTUAL REALITY MARKUP LANGUAGE)
A programming language that allows 3-D images to be displayed and manipulated on *Web page*s.

WAIS (WIDE AREA INFORMATION SERVERS)
A commercial software program that indexes large quantities of information. These indexes can be searched across *network*s such as the *World Wide Web*.

WEB BROWSER
A program used for viewing and accessing information on the *World Wide Web*. Netscape Navigator is an example of a Web browser.

WEB PAGE
A single page on a *Web site* that usually can display text, graphics, sound, video, animation, and interactive elements.

WEB SITE
Although this actually refers to a computer that stores *Web page*s, the term is commonly used as a synonym for a collection of *Web page*s.

WINSOCK
Software that acts as an interface between Windows Internet and *Internet* applications.

WORLD WIDE WEB
The collection of *Web site*s on the *Internet*. These sites are explored using *hypertext* links, which take you to other pages on the same site, or to pages on a different site.

Index

127

r=right, l=left, c=center, t=top,
a=above, b=below

The publisher would like to thank
the following for their kind permission to reproduce the photographs:
Cyberia Paris, one of Cyberia's
global chain of Internet cafés,
photo: Frederik Fourment: back
cover tl, 28bl; Robert Harding
Picture Library: Warren Faidley 16-
17; Nigel Francis 56-57, Jon Zioner
40-41; IBM: 12tr; The Image Bank:
94-95, Jay Brousseau, 94-95, Garry
Gay 16-17; NASA/JPL: back cover
tc, 13 tr,c,ca,cl, 42cr, 83cr, 84cl,
93cr; NCSA/UIUC: 12bl; Copyright
©1996 PhotoDisc, Inc.: 1, 2-3;
Tony Stone: Darrell Gulin 56-57,
Randy Wells 28t; Telegraph Colour
Library: 40-41, 46br, 80-81, 87cla;
Zefa Pictures: 8-9;

The publisher would like to thank
the following copyright holders for
their kind permission to reproduce
their screengrabs/products, all of
which are trademarks:
3DO, Studio 3DO, The 3DO logos
and Meridian59 are the trademarks
and/or registered trademarks of
the 3DO Company. ©The 3DO
Company. All rights reserved: 97br;
"AOL" and the AOL triangle logo
are registered trademarks of
America Online, Inc. All rights
reserved: 109c, b, 110, 113br;
©Lee Burton 68b; Center for Sea
Turtle Research, University of
Florida: 54bl; CERN: 102br;
Permission granted by CompuServe
Incorporated. Thank you to
CompuServe (Information Services)
UK for their help: 29cr, 106-107,

108br, 109tl, 111, 113cr,cb; Condé
Net/Condé Nast Publications, Inc.:
60tr; ©Digital Equipment
Corporation 1996: 77t,c,br, 78cla,
79b; ©1996 by Excite Inc.: 8cl,78cl;
Copyright ©1995, 1996 Forte
Advanced Management Software,
Inc. All Rights Reserved: front cover
crb, 43tr, 90-90, 92, 93ca, cr, br;
FTP Software, Worldwide: 45clb;
Fun City Technologies: 102bl;
©Globalscape, Inc.: 42bl, 44, 45t,
46c,b; The Multimedia Newsstand
is a service of the Hearst
Corporation. All Rights Reserved,
The Hearst Corporation: 59cra; Joe
Hines: 96c; Copyright ©Hollywood
Online Inc.: 59tcl; IDG Media/PC
Advisor: 29crb; Reprinted by per-
mission. Infoseek, Infoseek Guide,
Infoseek Personal and the Infoseek
logo are trademarks of Infoseek
Corporation which may be regis-
tered in certain jurisdictions.
Copyright ©1995, 1996 Infoseek
Corporation. All rights reserved.
78tc; IUMA: back cover cra, spine
c, 68clb; Jeff Kuhn: 77bl;
Copyright ©1996 Lycos, Inc.
All Rights Reserved. The Lycos©
"Catalog of the Internet." Copyright
©1994, 1995, 1996 Carnegie
Mellon University. All Rights
Reserved. Used by permission: 78c;
©1996 Macromedia Inc. All rights
reserved. Shockwave is a trademark
of Macromedia Inc.: 70, 71t; ©M/B
Interactive Inc. All Music by Akio
Akashi: 71b; mIRC Co.Ltd: 100-
101; MSN is a trademark, and
Microsoft, MS-DOS, and Windows
are registered trademarks of
Microsoft Corporation: 20cr, 21cl,

c,b, 23, 24,tl,tc,c,bl, 25tl,cl,bl,br,
27tr, 34-35, 36-37, 38, 39c,br, 55,
59c, 62-63, 68c, 72b, 74cr, 75cra,
crb, bc, 85t, 97tr,tra,ca, 108cr,bl,
112, 113ca,crb (Screen shots
reprinted with permission from
Microsoft Corporation); ©and® MTV
Networks. MTV and related marks
are trademarks of MTV Networks.
All rights reserved: 59crb; ©1996,
National Resource Council of
Canada (Institute for
Microstructural Sciences): 58bc;
Netscape Communications, the
Netscape Communications logo,
Netscape and Netscape Navigator
are trademarks of Netscape
Communications Corporation: front
cover cb, 14tr, 15tl,tr, 42clb, 43tl,
58cr, 59tr, 64-65, 66-67, 68bc,
72t, 74ca, 75tc,c,cb, 82b, 83t,c,bl,
85b, 86bl, 99tr, 102cl; NEUROGolf,
designed and developed by NEU-
ROTEC International Corp., Boston,
MA, USA, a subsidiary of NEU-
ROTEC Hochtechnologie GmbH,
Friedrichshafen, Germany.
NEUROGolf was developed using
Macromedia Director version 5.0
and runs using the Macromedia
Shockwave plug-in version 5.0
for Netscape Navigator: 96tr;
WinZip©Copyright ©1991-1996 by
Nico Mak Computing Inc. All rights
reserved: 116; NlightN: 78t;
Brandon Plewe: back cover crb,
11bl; PMC Consumer Electronics
Ltd: back cover bl, 18cb;
©Progressive Networks, All rights
reserved: 14cr, 15br, 68cb;
PsiNet UK Ltd: 29cr; Qualcomm
Incorporated: back cover cla, front
cover br, 50-51, 52, 53c,b; Walter

Shelby Group Ltd: 54cr,br;
Copyright ©1993-1996 Snappy
Software. Created by George H.
Silva: 117; ©1996, Superscape VR
plc: 69c,br; Teleport Internet
Services: 59br; ©UUNET PIPEX
1996: 45bl; ©Video On Line/
RadioX: 15bl; John Walker: 11tr;
Web Broadcasting Service ©1996
WebChat Communications Inc.
All Rights Reserved: 102br; Full
title to all copyrights are owned
by WebGenesis Inc. (607) 255-7724
USA: 102ca,c, 103cr; Web21 of
Palto Alto, California, makers of
the 100 hot Web sites, a distin-
guished directory of the Net, can
be reached at www.100hot.com:
78ct; David Woakes: 43br; Worlds
Chat Screen Grabs ©1996, Worlds
Inc.: front cover clb, 104-105;
©1996 WGN-TV: 11br, 59tcr; WRQ:
58tr, 59tcl; WSB-TV/Atlanta, Ga:
11ca, 59tl; Text and artwork copyright ©1996 by YAHOO! Inc. All
rights reserved. YAHOO! and the
YAHOO! logo are trademarks of
YAHOO! Inc.: 78ca, b.

The full names of certain products
referred to in this book are:
Microsoft® MS-DOS®,
Microsoft® Windows® 95,
MSN™, The Microsoft® Network,
Microsoft® Internet Gaming Zone,
Microsoft® Internet Explorer.

Every effort has been made
to trace the copyright holders.
The publisher apologizes for
any unintentional omissions and
would be pleased, in such cases,
to add an acknowledgement
in future editions.